OAKVILLE
A Small Town
1900-1930

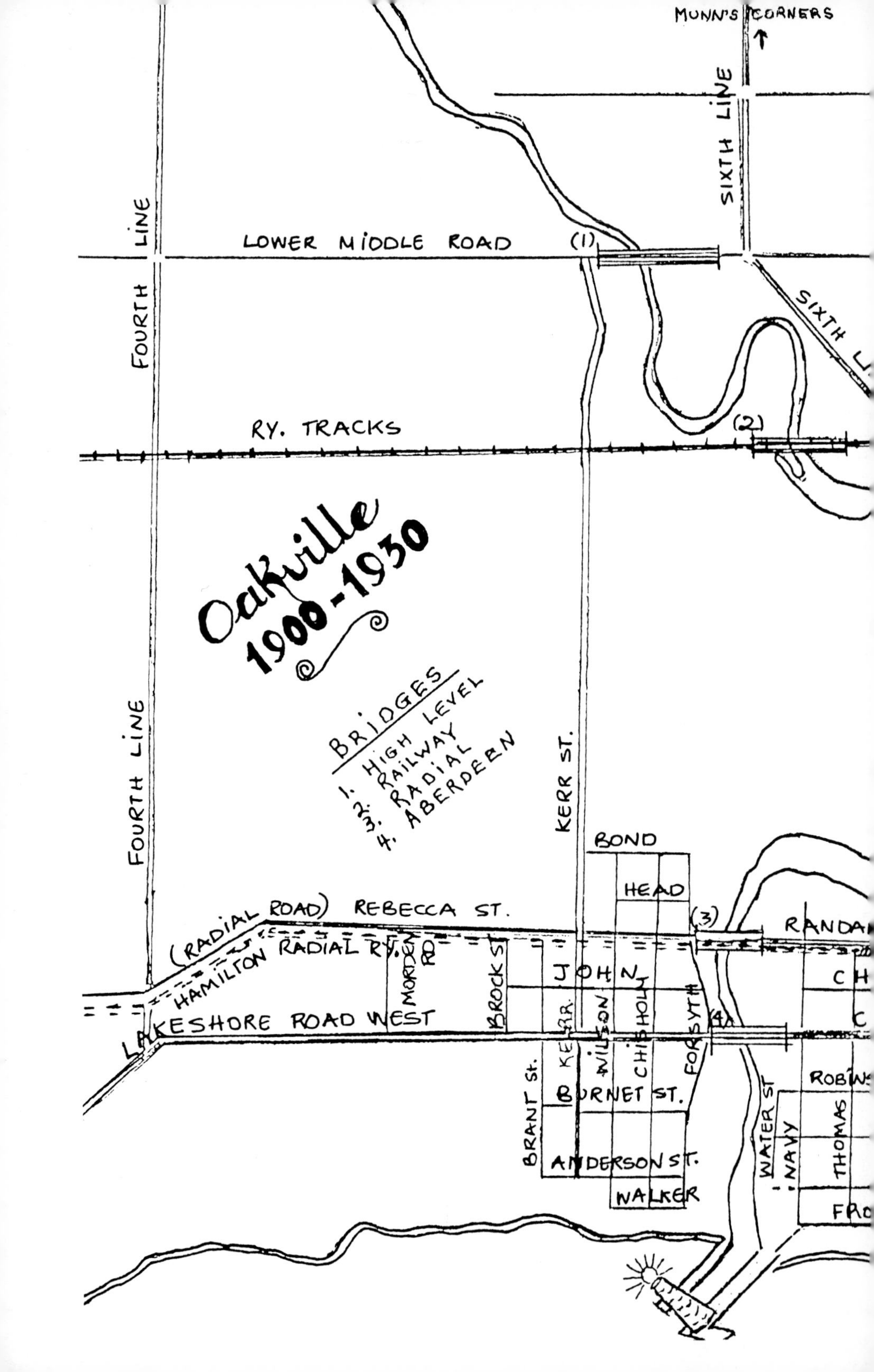

MUNN'S CORNERS
SIXTH LINE
LOWER MIDDLE ROAD
FOURTH LINE
(1)
SIXTH LINE
RY. TRACKS
(2)
Oakville
1900-1930
BRIDGES
1. HIGH LEVEL
2. RAILWAY
3. RADIAL
4. ABERDEEN
KERR ST.
BOND
HEAD
(RADIAL ROAD) REBECCA ST.
(3)
HAMILTON RADIAL RY.
MORDEN RD
BROCK ST
JOHN
LAKESHORE ROAD WEST
KERR
WILSON
CHISHOLM
FORSYTH
(4)
BRANT ST.
BURNET ST.
ANDERSON ST.
WALKER
WATER ST
NAVY
THOMAS

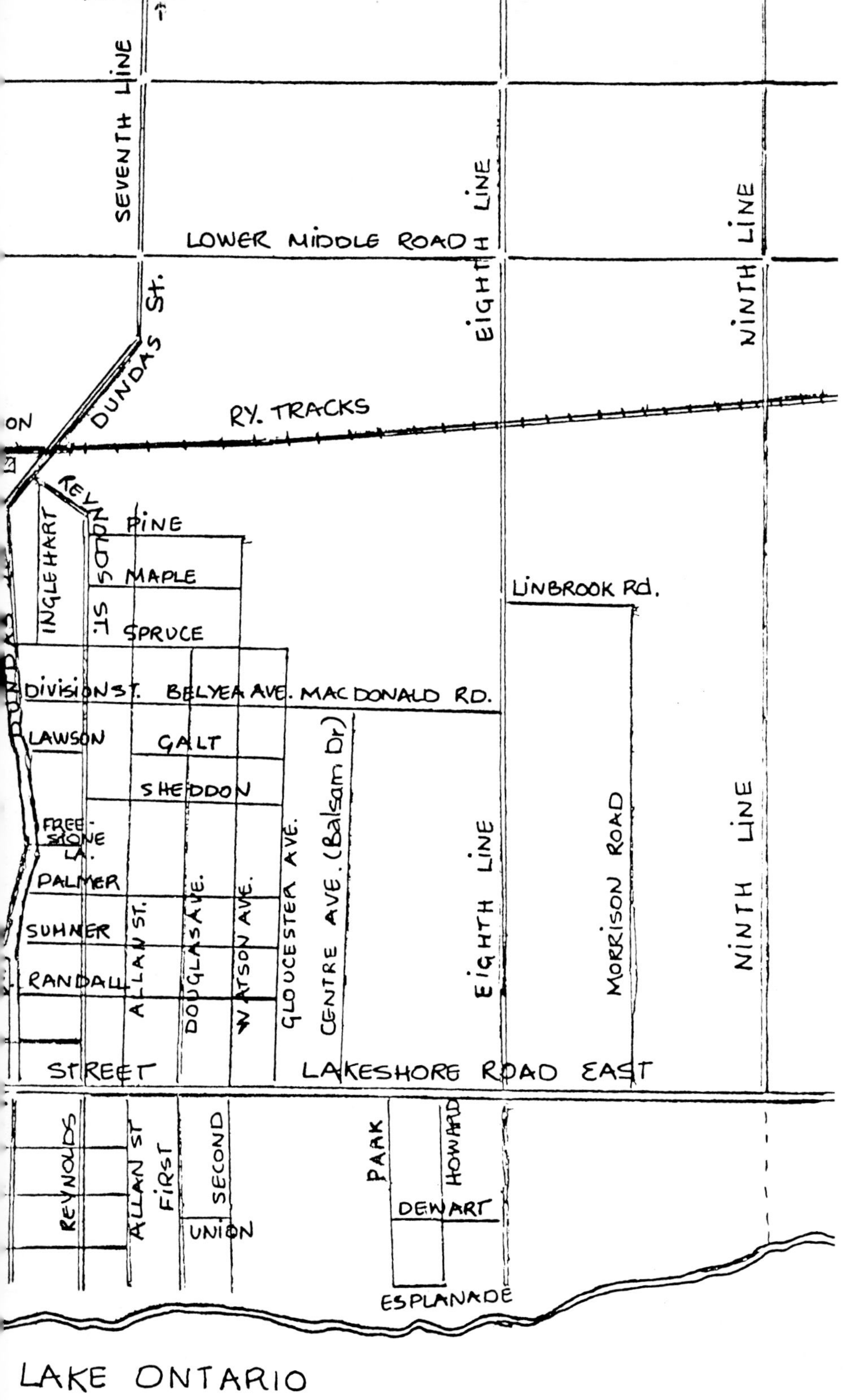

SEVENTH LINE
LOWER MIDDLE ROAD
EIGHTH LINE
NINTH LINE
DUNDAS St.
RY. TRACKS
ON
REYNOLDS ST.
INGLEHART
PINE
MAPLE
SPRUCE
LINBROOK Rd.
DIVISION ST.
BELYEA AVE.
MACDONALD RD.
LAWSON
GALT
SHEDDON
FREE-STONE LA.
PALMER
SUMNER
RANDALL
ALLAN ST.
DOUGLAS AVE.
WATSON AVE.
GLOUCESTER AVE.
CENTRE AVE. (Balsam Dr)
MORRISON ROAD
STREET
LAKESHORE ROAD EAST
REYNOLDS
ALLAN ST
FIRST
SECOND
UNION
PARK
HOWARD
DEWART
ESPLANADE
LAKE ONTARIO

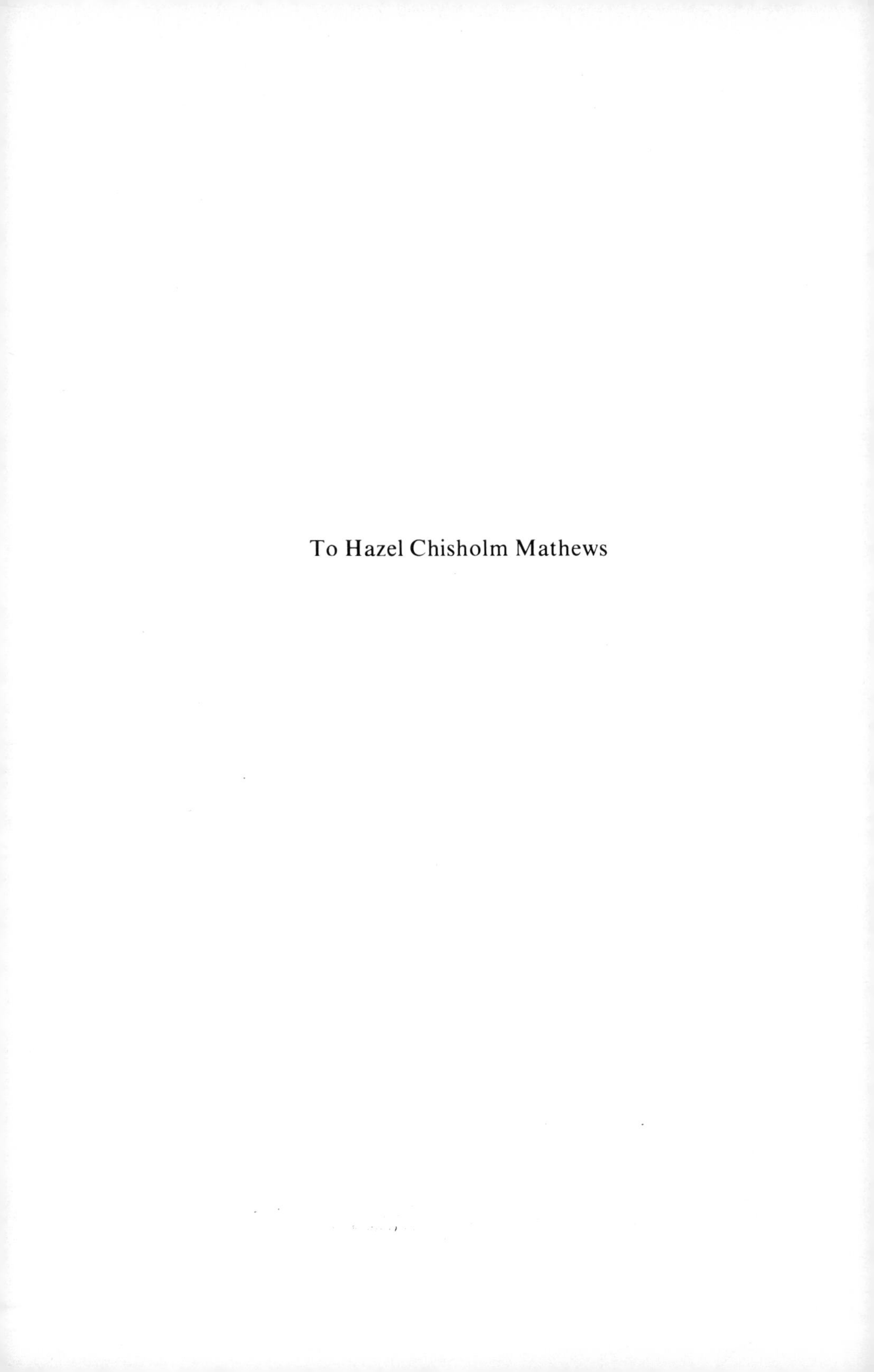

To Hazel Chisholm Mathews

OAKVILLE

A SMALL TOWN
1900-1930

FRANCES ROBIN AHERN

ISBN 0-919822-46-0

3rd Edition, February 1986
Edited by Dr. Mary P. Bentley

Back cover sketch of Oakville House by Angela Macdonald, courtesy of Harvey R. Goodbrand

Photographs supplied by the Photograph Collection of the Oakville Historical Society.

We especially wish to acknowledge the Ontario Heritage Foundation of the Ministry of Culture and Recreation, whose grant-in-aid of publication made this book possible.

Published by the Oakville Historical Society in association with
The Boston Mills Press
98 Main Street
Erin, Ontario

Contents

List of Plates

Frances Robin Ahern in 1931

Foreword

It is most appropriate that Frances Robin Ahern chose to write this delightful portrait of Oakville as a small town because she was present when many of the events described took place, in the years between 1900 and 1930.

During the many years that it has been my good fortune to have Fran as a close friend, and as an adviser when I worked on projects relating to Oakville, it has been a joy to listen to her reminisce about people, places, and events. Always amazed at the power of her recall with such vivid detail, I asked her how she remembered so many vignettes of her childhood days relating to her parents' contemporaries. She told me that her familiarity with her mother's friends and their homes was the result of her mother's anxiety concerning a small daughter's mile walk home alone from downtown in the late afternoons. School closed at four o'clock, and after the children enjoyed a short playtime with friends, the winter dusk would almost certainly be closing in.

Since her mother's afternoons were well occupied during the week, Fran was instructed to drop in wherever her mother happened to be, and they walked home together. The "Monday Club" began the week; the Women's Auxiliary at St. Jude's met every Tuesday; and Wednesdays, Thursdays, and Fridays would be taken up with Bridge, a "Tea," or a "Call." On arrival, she recalls sitting, like a statue, since little girls were encouraged "to be seen but not heard," drinking in every detail of dress, conversation, personalities, and surroundings, and enjoying generous offerings of cookies and other treats.

Fran can tell of houses long since "pushed over," describing for us architectural merits and beauty, and spur the imagination with details of her favourite stores, their proprietors and merchandise, as well as all the smells, sounds, and sights that pervaded to make life a constant invitation for her mind to lock away memories, now taken out to be shared not only with her contemporaries but with us all.

This book will be a delight and a source of valuable information for those who live in Oakville and the many visitors who come to explore and enjoy this beautiful historic area. The reader will be able to walk the downtown streets, book in hand, to relive the past and its happenings because Fran has taken care to include chapters on each of the principal streets stating locations with infinite detail. We are also given a glimpse into the many charming homes in the town, as well as the magnificent estates that line the Lakeshore.

A member of the Oakville Historical Society since its inception,

Frances Robin Ahern has been an ardent worker for its cause. As a director she held the positions of treasurer and membership secretary. She was also instrumental in the formation of one of the best photograph collections belonging to any historical society. She collated and edited the Oakville Historical Society newsletter for many years and is the author of the addendum to *Oakville and The Sixteen* by Hazel Mathews. When the Women's Auxiliary was formed she became a member of its executive and has participated in many of its projects. What follows is a personal look at the town and you are invited to enjoy her reminiscences and those of her friends.

June Hooey
for The Oakville Historical Society

Preface

In Hazel Mathews' widely read book *Oakville and The Sixteen*, published in Toronto in 1953, the history of Oakville in the 1800s and, to some extent into the 1900s, has been thoroughly covered. Hazel felt strongly, however, that it was important to record for posterity a picture of the pleasant and relaxing life enjoyed in Oakville — a well-known resort area after the turn of the century — and she decided upon the years 1900-30 to illustrate this. Oakville remained basically the same for a further 20 years, surviving with other towns both the Depression of the Thirties and the Second World War, before industrialization arrived to change the small town entirely and forever.

For her purpose, Hazel drew upon the reminiscences of Oakvillites who knew the town well in the years mentioned above, and was happy with the response and enthusiasm of those who were kind enough to communicate with her; unfortunately, however, failing eyesight began to interfere with her project. While visiting Hazel in her home in Shelburne, Nova Scotia, I was told of her plans for the contents of her intended book, and was flattered to be asked by her to write a chapter and to edit others.

To those without a knowledge of Oakville's history, it should be explained that Hazel Chisholm Mathews was a great-granddaughter of William Chisholm, the founder of Oakville in 1827. Through access to Chisholm family documents and papers, and through her inexhaustible research into archives, diaries, and other sources, Hazel Mathews produced the monumental history of Oakville referred to above, *Oakville and The Sixteen*.

Because her eyesight continued to fail progressively in the 1970s, no communication between Hazel and her friends would have been possible during the last years of her life had it not been for her daughter, Nancy Hart, whose love and patience in reading, re-reading, and taping correspondence from others, as well as whose expertise in photography, have made possible a number of the contributions on the following pages.

Upon Hazel's death, Nancy, aware of my familiarity with her mother's project and that I had known the town well from childhood, asked if I would complete the task, and I agreed. As a very young child, Frances Robin, I had come with my family to reside in Oakville. Over the decades I lived in a variety of locations, received most of my schooling in the town, and had a host of friends there. Later I was to work downtown for four years in the Canadian Bank of Commerce and, as a result, I had, as Nancy knew, come to know Oakville and its people very well.

Since it was Hazel's wish to record the period in somewhat of a personal manner, I hope that I have, with the others, been able to create the impression she intended. Sources of information have been first-hand familiarity with the town during 1900-30, both on my part and on the part of others who lived through those years. A few specific dates were found in our old family scrapbooks of random newspaper clippings; for references prior to 1900, I had need to go no further than Hazel Mathews' *Oakville and The Sixteen.*

I am very grateful to the Oakville Historical Society who agreed to undertake responsibility for the printing and publication of this material. My hope is that the contents will add to the reader's knowledge and enjoyment of the town. For ease in identifying the many locations mentioned, street numbers and names of today have been indicated. In the Appendix will be found the "Origin of Street Names" and, for reference, the churches, schools, banks, post offices, libraries, and customs offices listed in chronological order.

Lack of space unfortunately prevents the inclusion of many townspeople and locations equally deserving of mention: for all the residents, as well as the homes and businesses, however important or unimportant they may appear to have been, contributed in their own way to the charm of this "small town" of 1900-30.

Hazel was grateful, I know, to her cousin Dorothy (Chisholm) Souter; the Lightbourn family; the Hillmer family: Allan, Blanche (Robinson), Whitney, and the late Mary; Mary (Marlatt) Oliver; Evelyn (Urquhart) McCleary; Margaret (Armstrong) Munro; Dorothy (Byers) Sutton; Miss Augusta Jarvis; J. Douglas Wilson; and Robert M. Chapman. I join my thanks to the above and am grateful also to Mrs. Winifred Bedlington, the late Mrs. Agnes Forster, my ever helpful husband Arthur ("Curly"), and many others.

None of the material, however, would have appeared in print without the devoted and untiring perseverance of my good friend June Hooey.

Frances Robin Ahern
Oakville, Ontario
October, 1981

To Set the Scene

Pity the unfortunate North American Indian in the early years of settlement by the white man, as shipload after shipload brought French, English, Scottish, and Irish immigrants to their country. The new arrivals quickly removed the natives from their familiar sources of livelihood — hunting and fishing — and settled themselves along every navigable waterway they could find. In Upper Canada (Canada West) the inland waterway was soon taken up in large part by United Empire Loyalists, refugees from the United States who were given generous grants of land by the British government for their support, and the losses they sustained during the War of American Independence.

Surveyors were sent out by Great Britain to divide the north shore of Lake Ontario as evenly as possible into counties. These lands were taken up quickly, and the last two counties at the head of the lake were Wentworth and Halton, the latter named for Major Matthew Halton, secretary to Lieutenant Governor Francis Gore. Halton County consisted of four evenly divided townships, and it so happened that the two situated on the lake were opened for settlement shortly following the victory of Horatio Nelson at the Battle of Trafalgar. In commemoration, these two townships proudly bore the names Nelson and Trafalgar (now, however, changed to "Burlington" and "Oakville" respectively). The two townships in the northern half of the county were given the Indian names Nassagaweya and Esquesing. Within each township the roads running north and south were designated by the surveyor for the Crown as "Lines" (measured and numbered from one side of the township to the other), while those running east and west were named "Concessions" (also surveyed and numbered). This system was simplicity itself, making property and locations easy to identify, and stood the test of time from the early 1800s to the mid 1900s.

In 1827 William Chisholm, with his eye on the Township of Trafalgar, and in particular on the mouth of the Sixteen Mile Creek (then navigable) as an ideal site for a harbour and townsite, was able to purchase 960 acres of the former Mississauga Indian Reserve for $4,116 (New York currency), or $4.25 per acre. The rest is history — told superbly by Hazel Mathews in *Oakville and The Sixteen.* No further history of Oakville in its early years can be added. What follows is an attempt to show what Oakville had become, while still a small town, in 1900-30.

Oakville, situated in the Township of Trafalgar, became a village in 1827 and a town in 1857. The town grew and the boundaries between town and township in the early 1900s were as follows: on the east, the present Gloucester Avenue and Eighth Line South (Chartwell Road); the vicinity of St. Jude's Cemetery on the west; and on the north, the Lower Middle Road (Queen Elizabeth Way). Lakeshore Road became Colborne Street within the town limits, and on the east side remained residential as far as Knox Presbyterian Church. Throughout the business section — between Dundas (Trafalgar Road) and Navy streets — Colborne Street was referred to locally as "The Main Street". Across the river it reverted to the residential Colborne Street West as far as the western town limit. Sir John Colborne, lieutenant governor in the early 1830s, had been a distinguished general in the Napoleonic Wars, and many towns in Upper Canada had commemorated his name by using it for one of their principal streets. The name Colborne Street was not bestowed lightly. Without the lieutenant governor's interest and assistance in promoting better roads in the Country (in particular, the old lakeshore route), travel by stage-coach and other vehicles would have been impossible in most weathers.

CHANGES IN OAKVILLE STREET NAMES
(see Appendix, pp. 191-194)

Streets as shown on the "Plan of Oakville, October, 1835" and the names by which they are now known:

Anderson Street = Bath Street
Colborne Street = Lakeshore Road
Dundas Street = Trafalgar Road

Lower Middle Road = Queen Elizabeth Way
Sixth Line (south of tracks) = Old Mill Road
Sixth Line (north of tracks to QEW) = Lyons Lane
Seventh Line (north of Lower Middle Road = Trafalgar Road
Eighth Line (south of Q.E.W.) = Chartwell Road
Ninth Line (south of Hwy 122) = Maplegrove Drive
Tenth Line (county line between Halton & Peel) = Winston Churchill Blvd.

LATER IN THE 1900s

Centre Avenue = Balsam Drive
Division Street and Belyea Avenue = MacDonald Road

As Oakville grew, streets in the new "Surveys" were added (see Appendix, pp. 195-6). In the text street names that have been changed are given their present-day equivalents at the first mention in every chapter; for ease in identifying particular locations, modern street numbers are always given in parenthesis.

The Lighthouse, 1912.

1
"Beautiful Oakville"

At the turn of the century and after, several exceptionally attractive booklets, illustrated by photographs of the highest calibre, were produced to help promote the desirability of taking up residence in the "Beautiful Town of Oakville." One of the earliest of these, produced in 1898 by J.E. Commins,[1] was appropriately titled *Beautiful Oakville* and was distributed widely in Ontario. A glance at it, together with two or three subsequent descriptive booklets, proves beyond doubt the beauty of the town. Its title, then, seems a suitable one for our opening chapter.

Mr. Commins wrote enthusiastically about the delights of Oakville:

> "Where the Sixteen Mile Creek empties into Lake Ontario, forming an excellent harbour, and midway between Toronto and Hamilton, twenty miles from either of the two principal cities of the Province, is situated this charming summer resort, the subject of our sketch.
>
> "Oakville is an incorporated town with a population of about three thousand, and noted for its many natural attractions. . . .
>
> "On approaching the harbour the stranger is impressed with the beauty of the bright shingle beach backed up by green sloping terraces, and above all can be seen what appears to be a forest of Maples which line the broad and well-kept streets.
>
> "The streets are shaded by rows of maple trees, many of which were planted nearly half a century ago by men[2] to whose foresight Oakville is indebted for the reputation which it now enjoys of being one of the most beautiful and picturesque towns on the continent."

An impression, however brief, of Oakville as it appeared in the first one-third of the 20th century would surely have been one of a leisurely and pleasant place in which to live: a pretty, small town, whose residents very likely took for granted their lovely tree-lined streets and their enviable proximity to the lake. The number of fences throughout the town might have been noticed, and can be explained as a "left-over" from earlier times when the majority of households owned a horse, sometimes a cow, and possibly a few chickens. The fences worked both ways — keeping their own within bounds, and others' out!

"The lake" and "the creek" could be said to have been almost synonymous with "the town" in their effects upon it, both direct and indirect. We have been reminded often that the site for Oakville was chosen by William Chisholm for shipbuilding and trade, simply because of its situation on the lake and at the mouth of the Sixteen Mile Creek. One hundred years later this junction was still of great importance.

THE LAKE

The Oakville presented in these pages was very much aware of the presence of the lake. In those days men, women, and children used their streets constantly in walking to and from their destinations several times a day. This gave them rather a keener awareness than we have today of their surroundings and, incidentally, of one another! At the end of each street leading down to it, the lake gave walkers an enticing glimpse of its water: sometimes calm and brilliant blue; sometimes grey with its pounding waves during an east blow. The large town wharf and the harbour were still used constantly by private yachts, launches, sailboats, and a few excursion boats for Sunday-school and other picnics. Stonehookers* and freight-boats, such as those bringing coal and other commodities to the town, came and went. Dredges to keep the harbour open were in use quite regularly.

From the beach at Lakeside Park between Navy and Thomas streets, and at the foot of the majority of town streets, a pier, some of

*The stonehooker was a large "rake" made up of two heavy tines set at right angles to a long handle, and was carried on a flat scow. This rake dragged the lake bottom, loosening the stone and flagstone which was then brought to the surface, loaded on the scow, and transported to Toronto or other destinations for the building trade.

them 30 feet in length, ran out into the lake. These structures served primarily as breakwaters, and were also a convenience to many residents, who used them to moor their pleasure-boats and to enjoy the lake water generally. The piers were constructed mainly as huge timber cribs, weighted down with lake-stone and cement, and topped off with heavy planks. Although not built with such a purpose in mind, they were a godsend to the entire young population of the town, who used them all summer long as gathering-places for swimming, diving, merely "bathing," or stretching out in the sun.

From the foot of Dunn Street there ran out into the water the Lightbourns' pier, on either side of which was a pleasant, wide beach, and which was thus a popular place for bathing. The pier at the foot of Reynolds Street was seldom used by swimmers since the banks were awkward to negotiate, but the lake bottom here was mostly flagstone, which some preferred. At First Street Mr. Davis' pier on the west side was fenced off from the public; however, the Jaffrays' pier on the east side attracted many in the swimming season.

The high bank at Second Street posed rather a problem, but a long set of wooden stairs leading down to the pier was kept in good repair and many congregated there. In addition, those from the neighbourhood were generously allowed the use of a handsome and sturdy pier, built from the beach at the foot of the gardens of the present "Raymar," and many enjoyed their swimming and diving from this fine structure. Next came the Bacons' pier, in front of their house on the lakefront at the foot of Park Avenue (no. 10), and to the east lay what could be called the "resort area" of the town. The wide beach along the "Esplanade" was popular with all ages, including guests at the nearby Village Inn[3] and summer cottagers who had built here overlooking the lake.

In this vicinity the land between Lakeshore Road and the lake had been opened up early in the 1900s by the contractor Charles D. Carson for numerous summer cottages — as well as a number of good, permanent homes — and many families from Toronto and other points flocked there to live in a house near the lake. The popularity of this district was enhanced by the presence of the Village Inn, which stood on the east side of Howard Avenue a short distance up from the lake. An unusually attractive and commodious summer hotel, with 30 to 40 bedrooms and the usual wide verandahs affording a view of the lake, the Inn had its own fine tennis-courts, dance-floor, and dining-room. The fact that many visitors from Toronto were attracted regularly to the dining-room was good proof of the Inn's popularity since, before the highway was paved as far as Oakville in 1915, the drive from Toronto to Oakville and back, through the Lorne Park sand-hills and other questionable sections of the road, constituted something of an adventure! The Village Inn declined in use after the First World War, and was finally destroyed by fire in 1941.

The preceding paragraphs describe the lakefront in the town itself, but the same use of it was made by those who lived both to the east and to the west in the Township of Trafalgar. A fine pier was built by Appleby School, two miles west of The Sixteen, soon after its foundation in 1911.

In addition to providing recreation for the townspeople and others the lake indirectly played another important role, that of enticing several wealthy business men of Toronto and elsewhere to buy property along the lakefront, where they erected handsome houses, stables, and workmen's cottages, and beautifully landscaped the grounds leading down to the lake. So many appeared during the years 1900-30 that the lakefront came to be known, humorously, as "Millionaires' Row." Although much of this development did not take place in the town proper, but in the Township of Trafalgar, the effect on business generally was beneficial.

THE CREEK

Although the Sixteen Mile Creek no longer served the purpose for which it had been originally chosen by William Chisholm, it remained always in use, and a centre of attraction to the town. Yachts and sailboats were still being built during this period along the west flats below the Aberdeen Bridge. The two bridges crossed the creek where they do today: the one on Lakeshore Road was at the bottom of the slope; the Rebecca Street bridge, of "high-level" construction, stretched from the top of one river bank to the other. The bridge nearer the harbour, named "Aberdeen," was built as a swing bridge, but with the exception of the gala "Opening" in 1895 when it was photographed in the "swing" position, it was not again used in this way. Instead, shipping still moored below the bridge, which would, as things turned out, have had little opportunity to "swing," since the traffic over it continued steadily to increase. This narrow, two-lane bridge alone served all Lakeshore Road traffic, as well as the busy Marlatt and Armstrong Leather Company, whose many buildings spread as far as the lake along the greater length of Forsyth below Lakeshore Road. As well as the personnel concerned with the operation of the Tannery, the bridge carried across it the many commercial loads necessary for this

Aberdeen Bridge—Gala Opening

thriving business. As children, we never quite became accustomed to the sight of the many low-slung wagon-loads of raw hides, neatly piled "wrong-side-out," on their way over the bridge to be tanned.

Colborne Street (Lakeshore Road), from Navy Street to the bridge, was a very steep downhill slope, sometimes causing trouble to horses pulling a heavy load, or to the "new" automobiles that were beginning to appear in ever greater numbers. To the west of the bridge the road sloped more gradually but, until the Aberdeen Bridge was replaced at the end of the 1920s, a sidewalk of wooden slats with handrails ran along the south side of the road, both east and west of the bridge. Since the bridge was some 15 to 20 feet above the river water, these sidewalks were built up on trestles to bridge level over the marshy flats of the river. Handrails on both sides were obviously a necessity.

What is now the Anderson Bridge (opened in 1961 and now heavily used by motor traffic) was then used only for the purpose for which it had been built: namely, to carry the electric Radial Car back and forth between Hamilton and its terminal at Randall and Thomas streets. It also provided a useful "second crossing" for pedestrians from both sides of the river by means of a good sidewalk, well separated from and parallel to the car tracks.

Local yachts and sailboats moored in the river, as did those from outside the town particularly after the opening of the Oakville Club in

1908, when closely contested week-end races took place between Oakville and the other yacht clubs on the lake. Above the Aberdeen Bridge owners of launches, rowboats, and canoes made good use of the river for recreation, short excursions, and picnics on the two to three miles of water below the Railway Bridge north of town. Regattas were held frequently between the east and west piers at the mouth of the creek and in front of the Oakville Club. Swimming in the river was pleasant, particularly when the wind blew "off shore," turning Lake Ontario into liquid ice; a warmer swim in the river was then appreciated.

Although outside rinks and a good, covered skating-rink existed in the town, many preferred the creek, provided the "ice was good," and often skated as far up the river as the old Mill below the Railway Bridge. After a heavy snowfall, willing hands quickly shovelled off spaces on the creek for hockey-players or other skaters.

Ice formed very deeply in those years, the river water running free of the present problem of pollution. When the ice was considered to be at its thickest, long ice-saws were employed to cut square blocks of it for use the following summer in "ice-boxes" (the refrigeration of the time). The ice-cutting took place between the Aberdeen and Radial bridges, and the blocks were then stored in sawdust in the coal and ice dealers' warehouses on the east side of the river below Aberdeen Bridge, to be delivered house-to-house during the summer. "Lake Simcoe Ice" was brought in later to augment the supply.

Also stored along the river's edge was the coal needed for fuel in the town. Black mountains of coal, which had been unloaded from boats from Oswego and other ports on Lake Ontario, were piled separately as to variety and size for different uses. "Chestnut" and "pea" sizes were used in household furnaces, "cannel coal" in fireplaces, and "soft coal" for heating the larger buildings.

At the close of winter, the shallower upper water of the creek began to move again, and a loud "boom" was heard, often at night, when expansion caused the ice of the entire creek to explode into thousands of large ice-cakes, spreading from one bank to the other. This meant an end, for another year, to the favourite winter pleasure of skating for young and old.

SOUNDS OF OAKVILLE

Sounds played an important part in all small towns before the over-all noise of mechanism descended upon the world, and these sounds cannot be omitted from a description of Oakville in 1900-30 without its being incomplete.

The steam-whistle blown by the Tannery on the west bank of the creek sounded early each week-day morning calling company employees to work; again at the noon-hour; and again at five o'clock in the evening. The Tannery whistle was quite distinctive: rather low-pitched, with a hollow tone. The sound seemed unobtrusive enough but managed to carry to all parts of the town, regardless of wind direction, and was thus used as the official "alarm" in times of fire. The other regular whistle in town, that of the Oakville Basket Factory, was lighter in tone, with a slightly higher pitch, and was used for the same purpose. After the failure of the Tannery in 1924, the Basket Factory whistle became the "official fire-alarm."

The bells of St. Jude's and Knox Presbyterian churches were more than active on Sundays, and the bell tones were, and of course still are, quite distinctive from one another. For many years St. Jude's bells pealed half an hour before, and then a final bell, for each early Communion, Morning and Evening Service, and afternoon Sunday school, when held. The big bell, "Big Ted" (named after Edward VII with his permission), frequently tolled for the funeral of a well-known townsman or a public figure. St. Jude's chimes played morning and evening for 15 minutes before services, and the "changes" often rang gaily after a church wedding. I remember wakening early on Christmas mornings to the lovely sound of carols ringing out over the town, played on the chimes. The clock in St. Jude's tower rang each hour from 1907 on.

In cases of a serious fire in town the Tannery whistle was joined by St. Jude's and Knox Presbyterian bells, and in very extreme instances the Basket Factory joined in the alarm. All sounding together, these ensured a pretty complete turn-out of citizens to watch the ever-efficient fire-fighters at work, the crowd assuming almost the importance of a social gathering.

Trains, far more frequent then than now, blew their steam whistles (two long, two short) at all level crossings day and night, and rang their bells while standing at the station. These sounds were seldom noticed by day, and if heard at night had a welcome and reassuring ring, as one might sleepily try to guess where the train was bound for, and why passengers were not safely at home in bed!

Similarly, the sound of fog-horns from ships passing each other out on the lake made one stop and consider the weather conditions close to home. The electric Radial Car, arriving and leaving every hour to and from its terminal at Randall and Thomas streets, gave a rather musical "electric" whistle as it crossed the intersections and approached the station. In Winter the town rang with the sound of sleigh-bells worn by the horses, either in team, pulling a large four-runner sleigh, or singly, harnessed to a cutter. We all took this musical sound for granted at the time, but missed it after the noise of the motor car had taken its place.

Until the Oakville Public School (Central School) on Navy Street was demolished in the 1950s the school bell, hanging in the bell tower for so many years, was of major importance to pupils, but useful too as a time-guide for others. At a quarter to nine, the "First Bell" pealed out a brief warning to possible stragglers that the "Last Bell," announcing nine-o'clock school, was soon inevitably to ring. (Woe betide a latecomer.) Lunch-time was announced by a welcome clang at noon, when we all dashed off in every direction for home, regardless of distance, since food was not encouraged in the school building. A repetition of "First" and "Last" bells took place at 1:30 for the resumption of afternoon school, which came to an end with another peal at four o'clock.

Mr. Boocock, caretaker of the school, was to be thanked for his faithful performance as bell-ringer. He was the essence of punctuality and order, and I never saw or heard of anyone try to take advantage of him. Mr. Boocock commanded respect from his post in the central tower entrance-hall of the school. Bearded, and wearing overalls and a somewhat round-shaped fedora hat, he stood by the bell-rope, large "turnip-watch" in hand, ready for his next important assignment. An enormous hand-bell of polished brass was rung vigorously by him at the beginning and end of morning and afternoon recess. Between these duties, Mr.Boocock ceaselessly wielded a broom both inside and out, keeping up an appearance of cleanliness; this was not an easy task since the floors throughout the school were of unpolished wood, oiled. The historic school bell, part of the daily life of Oakville for 100 years, escaped demolition when the old Central School was torn down, and is preserved in New Central on Balsam Drive.

TOWN LIFE

Family life remained very close until the use of the motor car became widespread. Lacking mechanical diversions, young and old spent hours of their time at home: reading together; playing endless games of cards, checkers, dominoes, backgammon, and snakes and ladders; even engaging in conversation with one another; and those lucky enough to enjoy music, perhaps singing together around the piano.

The church held high priority in family life. Participating in its support and in all aspects of church life was generally felt, consciously or subconsciously, to be a duty and a privilege. (For a list of Oakville churches, see Appendix, p. 199.)

It would be wrong, however, to create the impression that Oakville, or the rest of the country, was something of a Utopia in 1900-30. This was many years before socialism, and "welfare" had not become a part of life. The head of the house, therefore, must leave no stone unturned to secure the best job he could find, striving continually to better himself, since there was no benevolent government standing ready to support him and his family.

Work was done manually then, and as a result there was a variety of available jobs. The factories were busy and employed many, and the vast number of farms in the district were always in need of extra hands. The town — having no machinery, at least early in the 1900s — kept many workers steadily employed all Winter keeping streets open and sidewalks and crossings clear of snow; during the rest of the year road maintenance, utility projects, and other jobs kept the "town men" occupied.

Necessarily, there were always poor families to be cared for. The churches considered the underprivileged to be part of their responsibility and took an active part in assisting them. One of the foremost goals of the Salvation Army, the service clubs, the I.O.D.E., and other charitable groups was to see to the welfare of the less fortunate. Several slum areas existed in parts of the town.

As there are to be found everywhere, there were many town "characters" between 1900 and 1930. However, in the interests of good taste and for fear of embarrassing possible descendants, they shall remain nameless!

To help to place the times in proper perspective, it could be mentioned that, until the end of the First World War, the following were yet unknown:

the zipper	red (enamel) fingernails
cellophane	women smoking in public
the cocktail party	crossword puzzles
radio broadcasts	drum majorettes

tourist cabins

However, after 1918 and on through the "Roaring Twenties" these and many, many other signs of modernization made their appearance, not the least of which was the beginning of the "talking-picture" and the radio.

LOCAL GOVERNMENT

The simplest of governing principles seem to have been in effect in 1900-30. The County of Halton was represented by the Halton County Council, with headquarters in its capital town, Milton: this body was responsible for legal and court proceedings, roads, and other matters affecting the whole county. The four townships — Nassagaweya, Esquesing, Nelson, and Trafalgar — elected their own township councils, comprised of reeve, deputy-reeve, and councillors, whose interest was the rural part of the county. Halton's towns — Acton, Burlington, Georgetown, Milton, and Oakville — each elected its own mayor, reeve, school board, water and light commissioner, and councillors; in their respective jurisdictions these officials enacted their own by-laws and in general kept a watchful eye on local affairs. By some stroke of good luck, or good management, Oakville has withstood the temptation of becoming a city. Long may it remain "The Town of Oakville."

"THE GREAT WAR"

The momentous event occurring in the first quarter of the 20th century was, of course, the First World War, or the "The Great War." This was a dreadful time of uncertainty about the future, anxiety for the present, and much personal worry and sadness.

Although many young men already belonged to or joined other regiments, the greater number of Oakville men went overseas with the 164th Battalion, Canadian Expeditionary Force, of the Halton and Dufferin Regiment. Mobilized on June 5, 1916, they trained at Camp Niagara and on April 11, 1917, moved overseas to join the 5th Canadian Division. When the troop train carried the men away from the Oakville Station, every citizen was on hand to wave them on their way. The 164th Battalion was subsequently broken up to provide reinforcements for units in France. The regimental colour and the King's colour were presented to the regiment in 1917 by the ladies of Halton and Dufferin counties, and are on display to this day in St. Jude's Church with the Honour Rolls. The War Memorial, in George's

"Farmerettes"—First World War

Square, lists 64 names of those who gave their lives from 1914 to 1918. The population of Oakville in 1914, the first year of the war, was slightly over 2,500.

A number of women, as well as men of the town who were over the enlisting age, took jobs in munition factories and other essential occupations in Toronto and Hamilton, filling the places of the enlisted men. Some travelled to factories in Hamilton by the Radial Car, others to either city by train. Ceaseless efforts were made to raise money to help in financing the Country's enormous war expenses. The sale of Victory Bonds was a priority, but each patriotic money-making scheme and entertainment devised by men, women or children contributed in its own way to the war effort and the Red Cross.

The Women's Patriotic League was organized to lend aid in any way possible. Its members raised money by staging performances in Victoria Hall[4] and by holding numerous "sales" of home-baked and home-made articles; they also busied themselves sending off to the soldiers and sailors parcels containing food, cigarettes, and a continuous supply of clothing for wear at sea and in the trenches and "no-man's-land" — hand-knitted khaki and navy-blue sweaters, socks, scarves, and "Balaclava helmets," made by themselves and others. Most children entered enthusiastically into the production of many varieties of entertainment (good and bad), charging admission

"Carry On", Victoria Hall, 1918

and handing in the proceeds to a war charity. Home-made lemonade (five cents a glass), candies, and cookies, for sale by the children in front of their homes, were at least attempts at helping!

Although it is agreed that "The Great War" brought nothing but harm to each and every one, it did have the effect of bringing townspeople closer together, binding them in sympathy for a common cause and in determination to "Keep the Home Fires Burning."

THE DEPRESSION

The Depression which followed the First World War was a tragic time for many, and one of the sad sights was the number of men passing by on trains, "riding the rails" in search of work. The unemployed living in small towns among friends, however, were more fortunate than the thousands out of work in the cities, who had to cope with "bread lines" and "soup-kitchens." Always there remained a few, either unable or unwilling to work, who became "knights of the road" or "tramps." Quite harmless, these men walked from town to town — locally along the Lakeshore Highway — carrying their few possessions, and dropping in wherever experience had shown them they might expect some semblance of a meal. Most carried a tin cup, which even the inhospitable could not refuse to fill up with hot tea — or perhaps soup!

I wonder how many remember George Graham, a familiar sight on the Lakeshore Highway for some years. A large man with a fine head of hair and a beard, he strode along at the side of the highway — in no one's way — and was a man of few words, except to say "please" and "thank you." We were treated to only two visits that I recall, when he chose to seat himself on our verandah steps at Reynolds and Lakeshore Road. He customarily wore three overcoats at a time, from Spring through to the Fall, and at close quarters one kept up-wind of him for olfactory reasons. George was an occasional guest in the Oakville Lock-up, and his winter quarters were in the Milton Jail. Others in similar circumstances were taken in during the Winter at the Scott Mission in Toronto, and like organizations in other cities.

Footnotes:

[1] J.E. Commins: photographer, publisher and owner of Commins' Music Hall on the northeast corner of Colborne and Dundas streets. In 1898, after four years, it was destroyed by fire (see p. 116).
[2] In particular, Mr. William Francis Romain (see p. 93).
[3] The Village Inn: built in 1912 and owned and operated by Mr. H.F. Harrison, formerly of the King Edward Hotel, Toronto ". . . fashioned after the old Country Inn of coaching days, but fitted with modern luxury . . . an ample garage for tourists' motors will be built in connection. . ." (G.A. Griffin, *Oakville Past and Present...* (Toronto, 1912), p. 37.)
[4] Victoria Hall: approximately opposite no.220 Reynolds Street.

The Grist Mill

2
Industries, 1900-1930

Fruit farming was of prime importance to the community in the years 1900-30, and the large quantity of fruit grown brought a good living to many farmers in town and township. The industry received a particular boost in the early 1900s, when the dependence on lake shipping for all of Oakville's produce changed to the use of rail, on the Grand Trunk (later C.N.) line. Trains carrying passengers and express, together with those carrying freight, totalled about 13 a day, and this excellent rail service through Oakville contributed substantially to the success of its industry in general, but particularly to that of farming, since produce must be moved to market by the fastest means possible. Until the completion of the Toronto-Hamilton Highway (Lakeshore) in 1918, and for some time afterwards, thousands upon thousands of quarts and bushels of fruit — in crates, baskets, and barrels — were shipped by rail from the Oakville Station each evening during the fruit season.

Apple, plum, cherry, and pear trees were everywhere to be seen, both in orchards and in the comparatively large back gardens of residents. Vineyards were also numerous, producing every variety of grape. A few who grew grapes on a large scale were: Mr. T.C. Hagaman, Sixth Line; Mr. Charles Cross, north of the Railway Station, whose farm can be identified by the present "Cross Avenue," which would have run through the middle of it; and Mr. H. Farrow on the Lower Middle Road West (Queen Elizabeth Way). There were many others.

Such small fruits as strawberries, raspberries, black-caps, thimbleberries, red and black currants, and gooseberries flourished on hundreds of acres of good farmland. Oakville strawberries, in particular, had early earned a high reputation for superior quality and size and, when a supply arrived in the city markets, vendors would advertise the fact by calling "OAKVILLE STRAWBERRIES! OAKVILLE STRAWBERRIES!" and the demand soon exceeded the supply.

A farmer with a large "patch" of fruit, or orchard, was very dependent upon his pickers and his hope was to have the help of "clean pickers" — those who left no fruit behind on the vine, bush, or tree, to be wasted. Many town "regulars" had a good reputation in this regard and were always welcome on the farm. Also in demand were itinerant Indian pickers, some of whom returned year after year to the same farmer. Older school boys and girls were keen to pick fruit as soon as school was over for the summer. As in the case of their elders, some did a much better job at it than others!

Oakville Basket Company

The Oakville Basket Factory was the direct result of the need for suitable containers to hold the copious and varied crops of easily perishable fruit, which had to be protected in the best way possible during transport to the city markets: up to the early 1900s by ship; through to the 1930s by rail; and later by road. A good deal of experimenting and manufacturing had taken place in the late 1800s by Mr. John Cross, the Chisholm brothers, and others, and the Basket Factory had a long history of changes of ownership, destruction by fire and rebuilding. Through it all, however, the supply was kept up to the farmers of the thousands of baskets without which their produce would not have reached their market in saleable condition.

In 1900 the Oakville Basket Factory was owned by the Freestone brothers and employed a sizable number of men. It was located on the bank of The Sixteen on what was then known as "the Basket Factory Hill" — the steep slope up Dundas Street (Trafalgar Road), north from Division Street (MacDonald Road). Logs brought in by nearby farmers were stacked along the river bank, and as time went by extended farther and farther down Dundas Street. The log piles were complained of as a public nuisance, since they caused sleighs to be overturned and brought injury to horses. Nevertheless, a company that manufactured nearly three-quarters of a million baskets yearly was unquestionably an asset to the town.

Within two hours after a log entered the veneering-room it would be turned into finished baskets. One operator was able to make up to 2,000 strawberry baskets per day, and the "gang" making fruit and grape baskets were turning them out at the rate of 250,000 per day. About one-third the total production of the plant was in bushel and half-bushel baskets and in vegetable hampers. The bushel baskets were used for apples, and were sold in Nova Scotia, Quebec, and Ontario, their largest sale being in southern Ontario.

Soon after the turn of the century J.M. Wallace and Davey Chapman bought the Basket Factory from the Freestone brothers. In 1927 Mr. Chapman sold his interest to Mr. Wallace, who then became sole owner. The factory had suffered a disastrous fire in 1920 in its location on Dundas Street and had been relocated farther north on the street, south of the railway tracks.

Robert M. Chapman of Oakville, son of Davey Chapman former owner of the Oakville Basket Factory and an employee there himself, remembers how the business was conducted:

> "The pint and quart berry boxes were made from basswood for the reason that this wood did not taint the fruit. These products were nailed by hand until a wire-stapling machine was secured later, following the fire of 1920, which again destroyed the factory on the river bank, and its rebuilding upon the present site. Soon the company was making six-and eleven-quart baskets, melon baskets, meat baskets for the meat-packing trade (which were used also as clothes-baskets), and smaller shopping-baskets with handles, known as picnic-baskets. Most of these products were made from hardwood logs (maple, birch, elm, beech, and white birch), soft wood being used only for the basket bottoms.
>
> "The writer was the log buyer for the company from 1925 to 1934.

Timber limits, or whole 'bushes,' were purchased, and men sent in to cut the timber. Only selected trees were cut — those that were straight and without knots or rot. It was therefore necessary to have a sawmill in conjunction with the operation to keep waste to a minimum. The average 'bush' would provide about 50 percent of material for the Basket Factory, the sawmill taking the balance.

"During the depression of the late 1920s all of this changed, and logs were bought from 'store-keepers' and jobbers in Ontario. The 'store-keepers' advanced credit on logs received and, in the spring and summer months, men from the Basket Factory would measure and cull them, and load them onto flat-cars. These logs were bought from Perth in the east to Grand Bend in the west and North Bay in the north, the Parry Sound district and Haliburton County being the principal regions during my time with the company. In earlier days, logs were loaded with a jin-pole docking line (or long chain); then a cable was used, with hooks and a team of horses; finally recourse was had to a motor-driven hoist, which, I believe, is still being used today.

"At Oakville, the logs were boiled so that men with axes could bark them. A machine was then used to peel and veneer them while they were still hot. Boiling was a dangerous operation before electric hoists came into use. The boiling tanks were located under the floor and covered with planks, which were removed when the logs were to be taken out. Thus an open space of boiling water was left into which a man might accidentally fall and the log solution made injuries very difficult to treat. The introduction of cement tanks raised above the ground, and electric hoists with large hooks to lift the logs from the boiling water, makes one wonder why this operation was ever done otherwise!

"Baskets were delivered by wagons fitted with very high racks, similar to hay-racks, and drawn by teams of horses. One of the writer's first jobs was to assist the driver in unloading the baskets at the fruit market on Front and Church streets in Toronto. We would leave Oakville at three o'clock in the morning, driving the load by team. After unloading, we returned the same day, reaching Oakville at about six o'clock at night. We took the next day off but were back again to Toronto the following day! I remember the Lorne Park hills, which were formed of very deep and soft sand. *Two* teams of horses would be needed here to pull the loads up these hills."

Another necessity for the shipping of the fruit were the large barrels required for packing apples. The cooperage of Mr. Charles McDermott worked busily to supply these barrels for the apple-growers; in 1903 his factory produced 15,000 of them. The building stood south of Colborne Street on the west side of Reynolds Street.

The presence of such vast quantities of fruit in the district led directly to the location of other allied industries here. Allan Hillmer has reminded me of the jam factories, cider mill, and wine factory.

In 1912 Mr. E. S. Glassco and his brother of Hamilton took over the premises of the Oakville Fruit Growers' Association, south of the railway tracks on the east side of the Sixth Line, and became well known as the producers of "Glassco's Jams and Jellies." These fine products were marketed widely for years throughout Ontario, Quebec, and the Maritimes. After the First World War Mr. George B. Jacobs, who had been head jam-maker at E.D. Smith's Jam Factory in Winona on the Niagara peninsula, opened his own operation in Oakville in a large shed-like building on the east creek bank, off Navy Street North. This rather make-shift building had been used to house Italian construction workers while the Toronto-Hamilton Highway was being paved, but served the purpose of getting Mr. Jacobs' business started on a paying basis. As his operation grew, he built in 1922 a large, cement-block jam factory on the north side of Randall, between Navy and Thomas streets. Here he and his sons produced "Jacobs' Jams" for many years.

Patterson's Cider Mill, which perfumed the autumn air in the process of cider-making, was located on the creek side of Dunn Street at the curve, just north of Randall Street. The stone foundation of the mill may still be seen behind the house on that corner. A short distance west on Randall, the Oakville Fruit Evaporating Company carried on its business of drying apples and fruit for marketing. In his wine factory south of the Railway Station Mr. H. M. Volz processed baskets and baskets of local grapes from the abundant crops of the district.

The agricultural potential of the area gave rise to still other enterprises. Douglas Gardens, the flourishing market garden and nursery operated by Mr. John L. Cavers, was situated on the east side of the Eighth Line (Chartwell Road), south of the railway tracks, and supplied excellent nursery stock throughout the growing season. Farmers of the Oakville area brought wagon-load after wagon-load of wheat to be ground into flour at the old grist mill on The Sixteen below the Railway Bridge. Owned and operated in 1900 by T.H. Ashbury and Sons, it was sold by them in 1927 and three years later was gutted by fire. This historic mill had been operating since the time of William Chisholm, having been built in 1827; the turn at the bottom of the "Third Crossing" is built over its original site.

Although their supply of timber in the early 1900s was rapidly decreasing through deforestation, farmers from the surrounding countryside found a ready market for their logs in the town lumber yards and planing mills. A good deal of building and development was taking place at that time. The "Carson Survey" between Park Avenue and the Eighth Line was undertaken in 1905, and in 1907 the "Brantwood Survey" began to take shape. In 1909 the "Inglehart Survey," north of Spruce Street and between Dundas and Reynolds streets, was planned; a year later "Tuxedo Park," north of Division Street and Belyea Avenue and from Reynolds to Watson Avenue, was laid out. The two latter developments had both been formed from the farmland of John A. Chisholm in that section. Many houses and buildings were also being built throughout the town.

Busy builders and contractors of that time such as Carson, Bradbury, Shaw Brothers, W.H. Hawkes, Thomas Shields, Blakelock Brothers, A.F. Ford, and others, employed large numbers of carpenters, bricklayers, plumbers, and other tradesmen, and created a lively business for the planing mills and builders suppliers. Among these enterprises were Carson and Sons Planing Mill (on the site of the parking-lot south of no.159 Trafalgar), Davis and Doty's Lumber Yard, with the Oakville Pressed Brick Works, north of the railway tracks on the west side of Dundas Steet, and Blakelock Brothers' Lumber Mill, on Randall Street (approximate present location, no.300).

The Marlatt and Armstrong Leather Company, whose buildings lay along the west river-bank on Forsyth Street South, and at the southwest corner of Navy and Colborne streets, was the town's largest factory, employing a great number of townspeople in its operations, from the tanning of raw hides through to the completion of finished products. The company manufactured fine quality leathers for auto and carriage tops and soft leather to cover the seats of the "new" motor cars. Its specialty, patent leather, as well as other lines of leather products, filled a great demand at the time.

Many people depended upon the Tannery for their livelihood and, this being the case, the impact of its failure in 1924 was to spread a sense of doom over the town. Bread-winners were thrown out of work and some were forced to move away to find employment wherever possible. Not only families but other businesses in the town suffered as a result of this tragedy. Bringing the situation constantly to mind was the unnatural silence of the familiar Tannery whistle, by which, either consciously or subconsciously, everyone had been guided for so many years.

In the 1890s success and failure had regularly followed one

another in attempts to provide electricity in the town. Poles had been erected to provide a street light at each intersection along Colborne Street (Lakeshore Road), and also in front of the churches. Equipment was set up in an old paint factory on the edge of the lake shore, at the foot of George Street (no.212 Front Street), where coal was used to generate power for public and private use.

During most of the early 1900s electricity was a spasmodic affair, and with each failure of the lights townspeople returned to using kerosene lamps. Finally, in 1909, a more reliable supply of current was obtained from the Cataract Power Company of Hamilton, and the small "electric light plant" on Front Street was no longer needed. Even the supply from the "Cataract" was not to be depended upon, however, and it often seemed to the frustrated citizen that with the first clap of thunder (some contended it was with the first drop of rain!) the power would fail again — usually at a most inopportune time. Kerosene lamps were still the old stand-by when this occurred. In my memory, when electricity failed and the organ at St. Jude's Church suddenly became silent, the faithful Cecil Gilleland was immediately on the scene to pump the long handle in the organ-loft, filling the bellows which, in their turn, supplied enough air to operate the organ once more. Power "outage" was a feature of the years 1900-30 — and later!

In 1911 the Ware Manufacturing Company built an aluminum factory immediately south of the railway tracks, at the head of Reynolds Street, and began production of what were advertised as "The only Aluminum Kitchen Utensils in the Dominion of Canada." The new company tried to expand too rapidly, however, and after a few years moved its machinery to smaller quarters, the former Carson and Sons Planing Mill on Dundas Street north of Randall, where it remained in business for more than 30 years under the ownership of Mr. Ernest A. Mairs. Its vacated factory building at the north end of Reynolds Street was then occupied by the Oak Tire & Rubber Company, which manufactured "Royal Oak Tires" and which was managed by Mr. Frank D. Law. Langmuir Paints & Varnishes Ltd. built a large plant nearby, just north of the railway tracks on the east side of Dundas Street, and distributed its fine products throughout Canada under the able management of Mr. James H. Hodge.

The gradual increase in the use of the automobile during this period caused a great change in the life-style of the townspeople — as, of course, everywhere in the world. Wm. Whitaker & Sons in time decreased their manufacture of carriages, turning to mechanical repairs to the "new" cars and taking on as well the agency for the Chrysler car. From 1911 Robin and Bath carried on the first agency and servicing for the Model T Ford for a number of years, on Colborne Street (nos.265-67 Lakeshore). They also had the agency for the Reo, the Maxwell, and the International Harvester truck.

A. & G. Hillmer's Livery Service also gave way to the trend and became completely motorized in 1914-15, using motor-buses and Model T Ford taxis, or "jitneys." At this time they expanded into automobile sales and service for the McLaughlin motor car, and later for the Model T Ford. Their sales room and parts department occupied their building on Colborne Street (no.145 Lakeshore), and they also operated a garage in their newly constructed building on Church Street (no.147). Automobile sales increased to such an extent that after a few years they sold their taxi service to Robert Stirling, who, with his family, carried on the tradition of dependability that the Hillmers had begun. Robert's son, Harold, later formed with Vernon Dynes the partnership Stirling-Dynes Auto Sales & Service, which served Oakville car owners for very many years.

Supplying fuel and ice was indeed of the greatest importance to everyone in town. These commodities were proficiently supplied by: Hillmer's Fuel & Ice Company, W. H. Morden Coal Company, C.A. McDermott's Coal & Ice Company, John E. Ford Coal Company, Frank H. Chisholm Coal Company. Most of the coal arrived by lake-boat and was stock-piled along the east bank of the river.

Shortly after the First World War Mr. Frederick Harris arrived from England, and built and operated the Frederick Harris Music Company (on the site that is now no.461 Trafalgar Road). This firm published every variety of sheet-music — classical, popular, church music, etc. — and its name is widely known in musical circles today.

Oakville had always been famous around the Great Lakes and elsewhere for the good quality of the large ships and schooners built there. Although by the 1900s these vessels had virtually disappeared as a result of the increasing popularity of the railway, the building of smaller craft continued to make a name for the town far and wide. Of particular renown, among all those who knew a good sailing-ship, was Captain James Andrew. Almost without exception, the winning yachts of the Royal Canadian Yacht Club were built by Captain Andrew. The *Canada* and *Invader* (winners of the Canada's Cup), and the *Crusader*, *Minota*, *Beaver*, *Strathcona*, *Aggie*, *Temeraire*, and many other yachts of international fame, came from his Oakville shipyard, situated on both sides of the river at the foot of William Street. As he advanced in years, Captain Andrew sold his shipyard in 1915. The excellent reputation of Oakville shipbuilding was carried on by others and has been maintained to this day.

3
The Fire-Fighters

From historical records it is clear that there has never been a shortage of brave and keen volunteer fire-fighters in Oakville. The sources for this chapter are the family of Alf Hillmer, fire chief from 1910 until his death in 1944, and Douglas Wilson, first full-time fire chief for the Town of Oakville from 1958 until his retirement in 1976. In both cases, their terms as fire chief constituted only a fraction of a lifetime of service as "Oakville fire fighters." (Information prior to 1900 comes from Hazel Mathews' *Oakville and the Sixteen.*)

Before 1854 water to fight fires was drawn from the wells and cisterns of houses by a little hand-pump. In that year the first fire-engine was bought at a cost of £100. Called the "Little Cataract," it was fitted with a leather hose, the joins held together with brass rivets. Some years later "The Phoenix" was bought second-hand from the City of Toronto, together with a reel, mounted on wheels, carrying 500 feet of fire-hose. This scanty fire-fighting equipment was all that existed in 1900.

In 1883 Oakville suffered a disastrous fire which swept away the south side of Colborne Street (Lakeshore Road) from Navy to Thomas streets, and nearly destroyed the rest of the business district. Two years after this catastrophe a warning fire-bell was placed on the Town Hall on the west side of Navy Street; space was later found to accommodate the fire-engines there, and a tower was erected on the roof for hanging the fire-hoses to dry.

In 1908-9 a water and sewage system was installed throughout the town. The reservoir was constructed near the lake, between Kerr and Wilson streets, on the west side of town. Here the water pumped from

Lake Ontario went through a filtration basin; it then passed over to the east side of the creek into a high standpipe, situated on the north side of Randall Street, near the west end of the present Fire Hall. This black "pipe," measuring 100 feet in height by 12 feet across, held the water in reserve for use by the town. The water from it flowed by natural gravity and, until its dismantling in the mid 1930s , the standpipe was kept pumped full at all times to provide for any extra pressure needed by the town, as in the case of a bad fire. The new water system also provided for fire hydrants at regular intervals along the streets, and firemen were for the first time, able to depend upon the use of their fire-hoses and pumper.

Oakville Fire Department, 1913

With an improved water supply, the time had come to organize fire department services; thus, on April 28, 1909, a meeting of the citizens to discuss the establishment of a volunteer brigade was held in the old Town Hall council chambers. At this meeting James Lister, of the Whitaker Wagon Works, was made temporary chief of the Oakville Fire Department. On his resignation the following year, the town council appointed Alfred Hillmer the new fire chief. This was a happy choice, since Mr. Hillmer, always held in the greatest respect, fulfilled the exacting position of fire chief with great ability for the next 34 years, until his death in 1944.

"Alf" Hillmer lived on Church Street (no.143) across from his livery stable, where horses were readily available to pull the equipment to a fire. When a fire was at any distance from the centre of town, the reels and ladder were pulled behind a horse-drawn bus. At the first sound of the fire-bell, the horses in the livery stable would rear and stamp in their stalls. Mrs. Hillmer has told how their family was so organized that, when an alarm was sounded, each member had a specific task to perform for "The Chief." While one pulled on his boots, another his rain-coat, and so on, he would be down the stairs in seconds, fully clothed.

When the Town Hall burned down in 1911, the fire department lost the only hose and reel it had, and the remaining equipment afterwards was kept in a shed behind the Temperance Hall (now Tim Horton Donuts) on Dundas Street. After the fire-bell on the Town Hall ceased functioning, the steam-whistle at the Marlatt and Armstrong Tannery officially sounded the alarm, blowing a long blast, followed by one, two, or three "hoots" to indicate which ward — 1,2,or 3 — the fire-reels and firemen should head for. When the whistle blew, volunteers dropped everything and dashed off to "grab" the fire-truck on its way to the blaze, sirens wailing. When the alarm sounded persistently I have seen, more than once, two faithful volunteers, Oswald Farmer and Harry Wiffen, tenor and bass members respectively of St. Jude's choir, slide surreptitiously from their seats to "do their duty" at the fire!

Being a volunteer fireman could never have been called an easy or lucrative task. To begin with, strict training was required, and one rather exacting qualification for some was the ability to climb on the outside ladder to the top of the 100-foot standpipe! Upon acceptance, each fireman had to supply his own uniform, and participate regularly in the training classes and practice runs of the brigade. Granted, the volunteer earned the sum of 75 cents for the former and 25 cents for attending the latter, as well as the sum of $1.00 for heeding the call to a fire. The grand total of his earnings was paid to each fireman once a year, during the Christman season.

Throughout the first decades of this century the firemen worked hard at raising money for their cause, and their popular "Firemen's Garden Party" in Victoria Park (now Wallace Park) was always one of the highlights of the summer's entertainment. In 1919 the Fire Brigade collected $1,500 towards a small Model T Ford chemical truck, to which the town council added $500. With the acquisition in 1923 of motorized fire- and hose-trucks, and a motorized pumper in 1929, the Oakville Fire Department became fully mechanized. Pull-box alarms had been introduced in 1922, and that same year a new brick Fire Hall was built on the north side of Church Street (no.181), where, for the first time, the Oakville Fire Department was housed in adequate quarters.

LANDMARK FIRES

This information is taken from the official records of the Town of Oakville Fire Department:

TOWN HALL and TRAMP HOUSE — Navy and William streets, site of the present Bowling Green.

Date - Nov. 4, 1911 4 a.m.

This building was completely destroyed and included in the fire were the only hose-reels belonging to the Fire Department. Only one brass nozzle was recovered from the ruins.

ST. JUDE'S CHURCH — Thomas Street

Date - Dec. 20, 1913

The main part of the church was gutted by fire, and many church records were destroyed.

THE OAKVILLE BASKET FACTORY — on the creek bank, west side of Dundas Street at Division Street (MacDonald Road.)

Date - March 20, 1920

This factory was owned by the Chapman family.

"MOUNT VERNON" - former home of John A. Chisholm, on the site now known as Lakeside Park.

Date - Dec. 26, 1928

This was a 3½-storey, frame-construction home with a large verandah overlooking the lake. This residence was occupied by the Coté family of Montreal at the time of the fire.

T.H. ASHBURY and SONS MILL — located beside the Sixteen Mile Creek, below the C.N.R. trestle bridge.

Date - Oct. 29, 1930

It was completely destroyed.

THE VILLAGE INN — located on Howard Avenue, south of Lakeshore Road East.

Date - Feb. 28, 1941

Large ,wooden ,frame-building with verandah all around. Completely destroyed.

THE GIBSON HOUSE — located on the southeast corner of Colborne and Thomas streets.

Date - Feb. 16, 1942

This was a 3-storey building and was operated as a hotel by the Gibson family.

THE KENDALL LEATHER CO. — located at the southwest corner of Colborne and Navy streets.

Date - Aug. 14, 1948

This was a 4-storey building of brick, operated as a tannery and owned by Mr. J.R. Kendall. Completely destroyed.

Kendall Leather Company Fire

Meeting the Train, Oakville Station

4
Oakville in Motion

After the turn of the century transportation was moving away more and more from lake travel, which up until then had been used during the season by visitors to the town, and even by commuters! The Grand Trunk (C.N.) Railway by this time provided 13 trains a day, and residents and merchants naturally took advantage of this excellent service. Since the railway tracks and station were located some distance north of the town, a good bus and livery service was of the utmost importance.

The name "Hillmer" has been associated in Oakville, since the 1800s, with service and accomplishment. Edward Hillmer (1837-1914) possessed exceptional foresight in several fields of endeavour, one of which was the livery business which he founded in the 1850s. Of his two sons who were partners in the livery (later automobile) business, Alfred was widely known for his thorough knowledge of horses; he was also the distinguished fire chief of the Oakville Fire Department for 34 years. George became M.P.P. for Halton County, and served as Reeve and Mayor of Oakville for more than one term. A younger brother, Arthur, was owner of Hillmer's Fuel & Ice Company, chairman of the Oakville Water and Light Commission for many years, and Oakville agent for the C.N. Express. Many descendants of Edward Hillmer have made names for themselves.

E. Allan Hillmer, assisted by his sister, Blanche (Hillmer) Robinson, describes the business of their father, Alfred:

"A large, well-operated bus and livery business was absolutely essential to the growth and well-being of a town such as Oakville, where the railway linking the town to Toronto on the east and Hamilton on the west was at least one mile from the centre of its business and residential section. The majority of commuters worked in Toronto; living in Oakville, they had no alternative but to travel back and forth by railway each day. A small proportion owned their own horse and conveyance, but many lived at least one mile, some up to two and even three miles, from the Station. Dependable transportation by horse-bus, buggy or, cutter* in the early 1900s was what made it possible for these commuters to live in Oakville and thus to contribute greatly to the growth of the town. The same was true for the many people who came to reside in Oakville during the summer, or vacationed there. These passengers, arriving by train, might be bound for one of the numerous summer cottages on the lakefront, so popular at the time, or to the large, luxury summer hotel, the Village Inn, on the east side of Howard Avenue near the lake. A large number of regular, annual visitors from out of town filled such popular, fine boarding-houses as "Miss Walsh's," at the southwest corner of Brant Street and the Lakeshore Road, and "Mrs. Smith's," at the southwest corner of Church and Dunn streets, each with its lovely garden and excellent meals.

"Before the advent of affordable and dependable personal automobiles, and before the paving of the Lakeshore Highway from Toronto to Oakville in 1915, commercial travellers and salesmen came by train to Oakville, staying at one of the local hotels. Those selling to farmers, or covering points such as Bronte, Palermo, and Postville (Trafalgar), hired a horse and buggy to cover this surrounding area. At least two sales*ladies*, selling their material direct to the farmer's wives, often hired a horse and buggy and driver. (This was a job that quite often fell to me, as a young boy, during the summer holidays.) The horse and wagon, laden with boys' trunks and belongings, was put to particularly heavy use at the beginning and end of each of the Appleby School terms.

"The livery stable on the south side of Church Street, half-way between Navy and Thomas streets, was composed of part of the original livery in Oakville, a section of which had been moved from a location on the south end of the school "common" (now Centennial Library) before Edward Hillmer bought it out, to remove all livery competition. It was at least 80 years old in 1930, the date of origin being 1850 or earlier.

"In the early 1900s Edward Hillmer owned and operated as many as five buses; these were all curtained vehicles for summer operation. At

*Buggy or cutter: one-horse-drawn vehicle for two passengers — the former four-wheeled, the latter on sleigh runners.

Hillmer Buses at the "Oakville House"

least two were needed for the normal daily runs in Summer. These had seats running down the length of both sides, with six persons per side sitting facing one another. The entrance was by way of a door at the rear, and oiled-canvas curtains attached to either side of the bus were rolled up or down depending upon the weather. The two winter sleigh-buses had similar seating arrangements and a rear entrance door. The body of the winter bus, however, was set much lower and was totally enclosed, with windows on both sides. The sleigh or runner assemblies on which the body was mounted produced a bus with an extremely low centre of gravity. This was vital to keep it from overturning in the high snow drifts and deep ruts left by inadequate or inefficient snow-ploughing. A coal-oil or kerosene lantern lighted the interior of the sleigh-buses, and the floor was covered with straw six inches deep for warmth.

"The driver of the sleigh-bus, on an open seat at the front of the bus, was totally exposed to the winter weather. He would wear the heaviest of woollen underwear, socks, and mitts, a sweater, and a suit-coat. He also wore the thickest of heavily lined fur coats, and large coon-skin gauntlets over his woollen mitts. Large clay bricks, heated beforehand and well wrapped in woollen cloth, helped to keep feet warm when the weather was bitterly cold. The fare from town to Railway Station was 15 cents one way and 25 cents for a round trip, when an aluminum token was given for the return ride.

"A thoroughly experienced and well-trained team of horses was used to draw each and every bus. For years, both before and after they took over the operation of the livery business from their father, each of Edward Hillmer's two eldest sons, Alf and George, had his own specially trained and dependable team. George's team, a pair of blacks, were 'Pete' and 'Doll;' Alf's were chestnuts, 'Shadeland' and 'Starling.' (An especial favourite of Alf's was 'Old Bill.' On one occasion when Alf had been away from the stables for a few days through illness, 'Old Bill' managed to get out of his stall and, crossing Church Street to the house, greeted Alf by rubbing his nose against the living-room window.)

"One bus covered the east side of town, the other the west half, while passengers living at a distance greater than two miles were picked up or delivered by horse and buggy (in the winter by horse and cutter). People north of the railway tracks were served by horse and buggy or cutter, and later by car (after the livery and bus business had been motorized), because the population was too small to support a bus operation.

"A livery business usually had the mail-handling contract from Post Office to Station and vice versa. Hillmer's had this contract. The Post Office, in Louis Coté's time (1904-37) on the north side of Colborne Street (no. 221 Lakeshore Road), was one full mile from the Grand Trunk (C.N.) Railway Station. If the outgoing mail was light, one of the buses drove it up to the Station and put it on the mail car, bringing the incoming mail back to the Post Office. However, the mail around 6:00 p.m. to Toronto, and especially the incoming mail at that time, was so heavy that a horse and large wagon — later a motor-truck and driver — were needed to handle it. (Again I speak from experience since this was an "after-school job.") In addition to many bags of mail, several large bundles of the *Toronto Evening Telegram* and the *Toronto Daily Star* were part of the incoming six o'clock mail. All newspapers in the early 1900s were transported by train, later by mail-wagon or truck. Included were the large copies of the *Sunday World* which Hillmer's handled for many years. (Each Sunday Captain Maurice Felan walked the several miles from his home on Lakeshore Road West (no.398) and back, to pick up his copy at the livery office!)"

Dorothy (Chisholm) Souter also has memories of Hillmer's livery service:

"I think Alf Hillmer drove the bus mostly, sometimes George. Two horses were driven from a wide seat at the front of the vehicle. The bus had a covered body, seats running along each side, and curtains that were let down on the sides when it rained.

"One would telephone Hillmer's — *number 9* — and ask for the bus to call in time for whatever train one was taking. The bus would arrive at the door and the driver would call "All-oo-ay" — or something that sounded like that — and we would climb in and be taken to the Station. In the Winter the bus was like a big box on runners, with seats along each side facing one another and straw on the floor. At night coal-oil lanterns were hung inside by the back-entrance door, and it was always exciting and mysterious to alight from "The Midnight Train" in the dark and climb into the dim interior of the bus for the ride home — to the jingle of the sleigh-bells.

"Sometimes my father would hire from Mr. Hillmer a horse-drawn victoria to take the family for a Sunday-afternoon outing. It might be to Bronte, when the road ran along the lake and there were quite high banks in places; at other times we drove towards Port Credit. I remember being terrified of the antics of the horses when they met an automobile on the sandy hills of Lorne Park. We had no use for motor cars!

"I recall being taken once for a ride in Mr. Christie Armstrong's chauffeur-driven automobile — I think a McLaughlin. The seats were of leather and so slippery that, since there were no doors on the car, I was afraid I would fall out! However, the automobile was in the capable hands of young Bill Hill, who later on was the popular owner of Hill's Grocery Store on the north side of Colborne, west of Dundas Street."

I myself remember that to a great extent "shank's mare" was relied upon to reach one's destination in the early 1900s, and this foot travel was quite satisfactory because the town was still of a comparatively compact nature. However, the horse-drawn buggy, cutter, or larger vehicle was used widely also, and the wonder is that more accidents did not occur. A horse was occasionally inclined to shy at some unexpected object, or balk at one of the unaccustomed automobiles usurping their usually quiet streets and roads, so that a "running away" with driver and vehicle in tow was not altogether an uncommon sight. A driver who had insufficient control of his animal might find himself pitched out into a soft roadside ditch, and possibly suffer a cracked rib or some other minor injury. In general, however, this method of transportation was reasonably safe.

When we first came to Oakville in 1906, living in what is now no. 1409 Lakeshore Road East, a horse-drawn buggy, cutter, phaeton or surrey* was used, depending upon road conditions and the number of

*Phaeton or surrey: a light, horse-drawn vehicle seating four, by means of one seat behind the other, each holding two people.

people. One of these would be drawn either by a rather spirited horse, "Prince," or by my father's favourite, "Billy." On an evening in late Spring my family had entertained at dinner the new Rector of St. Jude's Church, the Reverend L.W.B. Broughall (later Bishop of Niagara), who was known to his family and close friends as "Billy." (My father was not at that time on a first-name basis with Mr. Broughall.) Having said his adieux, the Rector seated himself beside my father for the trip back to the rectory in Oakville, a light rug thrown over his knees against the evening air. My father, assuming that all was now in order, said to his horse — in no uncertain tone, I'm sure — "Get-up, Billy" (the vernacular — "Gidyup"). Dear old "Billy" immediately put all four feet into action at this command. At the same moment, the Rector thinking that this order was for some reason directed to him, sprang to his feet also, which action nearly pitched the future Bishop of Niagara headfirst over the dashboard! (I am happy to say that this accident was averted and Mr. Broughall survived to live a useful and long life.)

Allan Hillmer recalls the motorization of his father's livery service:

> "During 1914 and 1915 Hillmer's bus and livery business became completely motorized, and a number of Model T taxis, or 'jitneys,' replaced buggies and cutters. The bus bodies were specially built — one mounted on a McLaughlin-Buick four-cylinder truck chassis, the other on a 'Republic.' But the function was the same: meeting every train from 7:00 a.m. to the last train at midnight, taking the growing number of commuters to the Railway Station, and bringing them and other travellers back downtown to Oakville at night.
>
> "During this time, the firm of A. and G. Hillmer built a large cement-block garage (no.147) on Church Street opposite the old livery stable. They also bought the large three-storey brick building south of the livery stable, on Colborne Street (no.145 Lakeshore), as an automobile sales room and parts department. They gave up a briefly held McLaughlin car franchise, taking on the Ford Motor contract to sell and service Model T cars, trucks, and tractors.
>
> "After 1915 the Lakeshore Highway was vastly improved by paving, and many people were buying automobiles. In fact, in a few years car sales expanded so rapidly that A. and G. Hillmer were forced to sell their motorized livery business in 1919. Robert Stirling and his family from Arthur, Ontario, operated their taxi and 'jitney' business for many years out of the west end of 'Sandy' MacDonald's former blacksmith shop on Colborne Street (directly west of nos. 265-67

Hillmer's Motorized Bus Service

Lakeshore). (As a point of interest, blacksmiths generally became the first automobile mechanics in this transition, just as livery owners became the first car dealers.)

"Alf and George Hillmer continued in the business of selling transportation to the Oakville public until 1930, as Hillmer's had done since the 1850s. Instead of a 'service' the firm now sold cars directly to the people, so that they could own and operate their own means of transporting themselves. However, the end result was the same: helping commuters to travel back and forth to their jobs in Toronto and Hamilton while still living in the growing and constantly expanding town of Oakville.

"The horse-bus and livery-stable business, slowly changing and evolving, was a mighty factor in the growth, expansion, and importance of many small towns throughout Ontario and across Canada. As the railways linked the outskirts of towns, so the livery business linked the railways to the 'centres' of the towns."

Hazel C. Mathews recalls that her cousin, Allan S. Chisholm, was owner of the first car in Oakville.

"The owner of the first car in Oakville was Allan S. Chisholm (1866-1918). Born at 'Erchless' on the lakefront at the foot of Navy Street, he was a son of R.K. Chisholm and a grandson of William, Oakville's founder. While his brothers left home to seek their fortunes elsewhere, Allan remained at home as head of the family. He was a great sailor and, when Oakville was the destination of the Royal Canadian Yacht Club races, the yachtsmen were entertained at Erchless in large numbers, before the founding of the Oakville Club.

"It was Allan Chisholm who, by planting trees and spectacular flower beds of cannas, castor-oil plants, and salvia along the curving driveway he had laid out, developed Erchless into one of the show-places in the town. Being enthusiastic about working with wood, he made the great gates which hang at the north end of the property, as well as many pieces of the heavy 'mission' furniture so popular at the period. He was also fond of well-bred horses, and had a great respect for Mr. Alf Hillmer and his great knowledge in this field.

"It was for Allan S. Chisholm that the writer of the following narrative, E.Allan Hillmer, was named."

Allan Hillmer remembers a ride in Oakville's first automobile:

"It was, I think, about 1909 or 1910, and there were no cars that I recall in Oakville at the time. Horses and buggies were still very much the rule. My sister Blanche and I were on the lawn in front of our home on Church Street (no.143) when, coming north on Navy Street, appeared the first automobile I had ever seen in my life. Turning right onto Church Street, it pulled over onto the left-hand side of the street and stopped opposite our lawn. Out from behind the steering-wheel stepped a very handsome man, dressed in the complete garb of a motorist of those early days. He wore a long khaki coat, or 'duster,' a pair of brown leather leggings, and a motoring cap of the same colour, with a black peak; a pair of goggles was perched up on the hat-band above the peak. He also wore a pair of motoring gloves with large cuffs extending half-way to the elbows.

"As I remember, this handsome man had a mustache and a well-trimmed beard. It was none other than Mr. Allan Chisholm, a friend of my father's, after whom I had been named. Although my father, Alf Hillmer, had been very ill for a second time with typhoid fever, he managed to appear on the lawn, followed by my sister Mary and my mother. The whole five of us stood goggle-eyed, staring at this so-called 'horseless carriage.' To us it appeared big, very shiny, and beautiful — but strange.

"It was a large touring-car with the top up, black in colour, as I remember, with light-coloured wheels. Two doors were at the rear seats

— but none at the front. The gear-shift and the hand-brake, both brass, were mounted outboard on the left side, easily accessible to the driver's left hand. Placed high up was a two-piece windshield, with stabilizing rods running from the top corners down to the brass headlamps in front. These large headlamps, I believe, were operated from a carbide tank. The engine hood, or bonnet, had flat and angular, rather than rounded, lines, and the seats were upholstered in soft leather, those in front shaped to fit the contours of their occupants.

"All of a sudden Allan Chisholm said, 'How would you like to go for a ride?' He was lucky not to have been injured in the rush! My father got in beside Allan Chisholm, who was behind the wheel. My mother, Mary, Blanche, and I climbed into the back and stood up, hanging on to the front seat. I cannot remember how many cylinders this car was equipped with — or whether or not it had to be cranked, since on this occasion the engine had been left idling.

"Suddenly we were off — travelling east on Church Street in a cloud of dust! Several men stood watching and waving in front of the livery stable. As we passed the corner of Church and Thomas streets, Louis Kemp's daughters looked up from working in their garden on the southeast corner when they heard the noise of the exhaust, and stood still, staring. All along Church Street, people walking simply stared in amazement. We went around several blocks, and everyone we passed stopped whatever they were doing to have a look. Fortunately we did not pass one horse-drawn vehicle, so we were spared any trouble with 'balking' horses.

"Back we came onto Church Street, clouds of dust swirling up behind us, slowed down, and stopped where we had started from. As we got out, while thanking Allan Chisholm, the dust billowing around us, we understood why the driver was dressed as he was in coat, cap, leggings, and gloves! My father, still weak from his long illness, was wiping the tears from his eyes caused by the wind when I heard Allan Chisholm say: 'We were only going between ten and fifteen miles per hour, Alf.'

"My dad, who loved horses, actually despised the first cars. When 'Goby' Flood told him that they could be the thing of the future, my dad vowed that 'old Dobbin' would kick them right off the road. However, he lived to both sell and repair automobiles for a long time."

THE ELECTRIC RADIAL CAR

An alternative method of travel to and from Hamilton in the early

Radial Car at Station, 1908

1900s was provided hourly by an electrically powered car, operated by the Hamilton Radial Railway. The electric car maintained a shuttle service between Hamilton and Oakville, on tracks which, through Oakville, ran along what is now Rebecca Street as far as The Sixteen. Completion of the Radial Bridge (now Anderson Bridge) in 1906 allowed the electric cars to continue along Randall Street to the Radial Terminal, which contained a generator to supply the electric power needed for the cars. This building still stands at the southeast corner of Randall and Thomas streets (no.139 Randall).

The Radial Car made good time on its trip since the tracks were laid in an almost direct line for the greater part of the run to Hamilton. Leaving Oakville, the car would make stops, if necessary, at "Morden's" (Morden Road), "McCraney's Corners" (Fourth Line), "Ribble's" (Third Line), and so on. The tracks continued along Rebecca Street (which in those days was merely the railway's right of way and which became, after the tracks were removed, Radial Road) until they reached the Bronte River, where the Hamilton Radial Railway had also built a bridge, and then on through Burlington to Hamilton.

The ride was very smooth, the cars furnished with comfortable straw-woven seats, and this service was very popular and used extensively by persons travelling to Bronte, Burlington, Hamilton,

Radial Car Crossing Bridge, c.1912

and points in between. Many students living west of the town who attended the Oakville High School regularly used the service, as did the day-boys travelling to Appleby School, who got off and on "the Radial" every day at McCraney's Corners. Its low-pitched, distinctive whistle gave would-be passengers a fair warning of its approach, and drivers soon learned to stop at the level crossings.

The plan had been to continue the Radial line through to Toronto, and for many years a forlorn set of unused tracks was to be seen along Randall Street as far as Reynolds. The development and popularity of the automobile, I understand, put an end to this plan. Radial service to Oakville terminated in 1924.

THE LAKESHORE BUS

Before the paving of the Toronto-Hamilton Highway a journey to Toronto by the Lakeshore Road was not to be undertaken lightly. The road surface itself was rather indifferent, to say the least, quite apart from the two or three steep sand-hills that were located east of Clarkson and through Lorne Park. A common sight was a "casualty of the road" with a flat tire, an overheated motor, or possibly something worse! However, when the paving of the Lakeshore Highway was completed to Hamilton in 1918, two competing bus lines gave a regular service between that city and Toronto: one began in the form of large seven-passenger limousine and became the Blue Bird Bus Line; the other was the Lakeshore Motor Bus Line (sometimes called "The Yellow Bus").

The ride to Toronto or Hamilton was rather tedious since the buses stopped, of necessity, to pick up and let off passengers at every pillar and post, but they gave very regular and satisfactory service on the whole. A "Ten-Trip Ticket" between Toronto and Oakville cost $4.00. The trip to either city from Oakville would take slightly over one hour, but the service was a great convenience to everyone along the lakeshore, especially to those who lived nearer to the Lakeshore Highway than to the Railway Station. Passengers residing on the Lakeshore Road considered themselves lucky when they found a particular Lakeshore Bus driver, Jack Harker, to be at the wheel since he would kindly, and with a smile, let me and others of his acquaintance off right at our front doors!

THE COMMUTERS

Commuters were then, as they are today, an important part of town life, but travel in the early 1900s was almost entirely by rail. As mentioned earlier, Grand Trunk (C.N.) Railway trains ran frequently all day, from early morning until "The Midnight Train," which left the Toronto Union Station at 11:45 p.m., arriving in Oakville at 12:45 a.m. As always, the faithful Hillmer buses, and later "jitneys" and taxis, were drawn up waiting for the late arrivals on "The Midnight."

Year after year business men, women, and students commuting to schools and university in Toronto, after a walk in many cases of a mile or more, converged on the old Oakville Railway Station (then situated on the south side of the tracks). When the train could be heard crossing the Railway Bridge over The Sixteen in the mornings, the walk more often than not ended in a "sprint" to the platform. The Hillmer transportation service was used regularly by many. Occasionally, before and after the 1920s, a select few might be driven to the train by a chauffeur; or a husband might be dropped off at the platform from the family car by a sleepy wife, wearing a coat thrown on over her nightgown because of the early hour! At any rate, a parking problem did not exist, since one car per family was pretty generally the limit.

The time-table for Grand Trunk Railway trains varied little year by year. Those used by commuters left the Oakville Station regularly

"The Commuters", c.1912

at 7:35 and 8:01 a.m., departing Toronto in the afternoon at 4:15, 5:20, and 6:05. Other regular trains ran throughout the remainder of the day and evening at convenient hours. Waiting for the train, passengers usually stood chatting to one another, spread out from one end of the long platform to the other, but after a cold winter walk to catch the train they crowded inside the Station to stand as close as possible to the pot-bellied stove in the middle of the waiting-room. Commuters became very good friends after a few years of travelling together twice a day for five, and often six, days a week all year round, and many a practical joke was conjured up to play on the unsuspecting, to relieve the monotony. Several "card fiends" played Bridge back and forth to Toronto every day year after year, a few of whom were E.T. Lightbourn, D.O. ("Doc") Cameron, Hubert Chisholm, J.A. Robertson, Stuart Brown, Ban Taylor, and Frank Worrell.

Commuters formed favourites among the train conductors, who plodded up and down the aisles of the swaying coaches, punching the passengers' tickets morning and evening and generally keeping an eye on things. The commuter's ticket was frequently stuck into his hat-band, leaving the passenger free for his newspaper, his game of Bridge, or an argument, while the conductor removed, punched, and replaced it with no interruption! Many a weary commuter, taking forty winks after a long day's work in the city, has been jolted awake at his own station by an alert conductor, thus being saved the dreaded inconvenience of being carried on to the next station. Mr. Johnson, in his neat uniform and cap, his hair turned white in the service of the Grand Trunk Railway Company, was one of many fine conductors of that time.

The very early rail coaches were lighted first by gas and later by rather dim electric light. The high seat-backs could be adjusted to accommodate either two or four to a seat and were covered in a sturdy green plush, with a small "sculptured" pattern. Each of the long coaches contained a separate smoking-compartment at one end, a washroom, and a tap, supplying cold water beside which hung a cylinder of wax cups. Although the many coaches were held together with couplings, these were protected from the outside, and it was possible to pass safely from one coach to another. A book of "Ten-Trip Tickets" cost $2.50; the "Fifty-Ride Ticket," punched during each ride by the conductor, cost $8.35. The latter was calculated to last for one month of commuting.

The Grand Trunk Railway System was the owner of the right of way through Oakville. C.P.R. trains were allowed use of these tracks but only freight-trains, and not those carrying passengers were allowed stops along the line. The C.P.R. passenger-train was known as "The Flyer." With no stops made between Hamilton and Toronto, these thundering trains (coaches and freight-cars always coloured dark red) would pick up considerable speed and, when one of them was spotted approaching in the distance, someone among those waiting on the platform would shout: "Here comes The Flyer" — and we all would hold our hats and close our eyes against the cinders which lay thickly along the tracks, a by-product of the coal-burning steam-engines of the day.

SHIPPING

Ships carrying passengers and freight, such as the *Macassa*, *Modjeska*, *Corona*, *Turbinia*, and others, which in the late 1800s made regular stops at Oakville on their runs between Toronto and Hamilton, by-passed Oakville during the early 1900s and could be seen moving past, and their whistles occasionally heard, some distance out on the lake. Although Oakville had been known around the lake as a bustling commercial port, lake transportation had all but given way to the railroad, which now was used to move a great percentage of the farm produce and other commodities to the city markets.

The *White Star*, owned by the Oakville Navigation Company, continued carrying freight, was also a popular boat for excursions, and could be chartered for Sunday-school picnics and other outings. An L-shaped addition was built at the east end of the Oakville pier, so that passengers could be taken on or discharged without the necessity of mooring in the harbour. Unfortunately, the *White Star* burned at her moorings in the Toronto harbour and, although attempts were made to continue shipping fruit by smaller freight-boats, farmers, in the end, chose the railway. Although put to a different use today, the Oakville harbour is still enjoyed by many with pleasure-boats of every description.

Wm. Whitaker & Sons

5
Dundas Street
Trafalgar Road

Oakville's Dundas Street was officially so named on the very first map of Oakville in 1835. It soon developed into an important street as far north as George's Square, but beyond this a winding road, referred to as "the River Road," followed the bank of The Sixteen to the Sixth Line (Old Mill Road), where it branched off in a "Y" to join the Seventh Line (Trafalgar Road) at the town limit, the Lower Middle Road (Queen Elizabeth Way). The northern part of town then was undeveloped except for farmlands owned by the Chisholm family.

In early days, before the railway came, Oakville was completely dependent for its mail upon the stage-coach, which ran from Toronto to the village of Dundas, along what was known later as "the Dundas Highway" (Highway no. 5). This stage-coach delivered and picked up the mail for Oakville at the crossroads of the Seventh Line (the old village of Postville).[1] The mail was carried between this point and the town either by horse-drawn vehicle or horseback by way of the Seventh Line, which was, except in the dead of winter, sometimes impassable for those using it, particularly in bad weather on the ascent or descent of "the Red Hill."

The Red Hill[2] is the name by which the ridge or escarpment just north of Oakville has always been known, and its name derives from the heavy red clay of which it and a great deal of the land in its vicinity is composed. The clay, when wet or even damp, is unbelievably slippery and affords no traction whatsoever to a wheeled vehicle. Many attempts were made year after year in the early days to build corduroy or plank roads up the Seventh Line, but, because of the unusually heavy clay soil, these attempts were far from successful for a long time to come.

It can well be understood, then, that when the railway was put through one mile north of Oakville during the latter half of the 1800s, it was welcomed as the town's salvation, involving as it did a mere one-mile trip from the Post Office to the Oakville Station to deliver and pick up the mail. Not only the mail came and went by rail, but also an ever-increasing range of fruit, food, vegetables, and merchandise of all kinds and, of course, many, many people. The never-ending task of carrying these people to and from the Station is described in the chapter "Oakville in Motion."

After the arrival of the railway, Dundas Street was extended from George's Square up to the tracks and was soon spoken of familiarly as "the Station Road" for its importance in connecting the downtown to its main communication with the outside world, the railway at the Oakville Station. From that time on, Dundas Street became gradually a fashionable street with many fine houses. E. Allan Hillmer recalls its development:

> "The Station Road was at first a dirt road. Then some crushed stone was scattered over it and rolled with a steam-roller. Later, Tarvia was sprinkled heavily over the crushed stone and the whole rolled down until it was smooth. Around the time of the First World War the road was paved with concrete, but when the large cement 25-foot squares were laid, each was separated from the next by a strip of steel to allow for expansion. This was a good idea in the wrong place. Over the years the concrete between the steel dividing-joints wore down in the centre, leaving the steel cross-joints at their original level. The result was a hump which failed to wear down, so that every 25 feet the wheels of buses, Ford Model T taxies, 'jitneys,' trucks, and private vehicles struck a bump, rather to the discomfort of passengers travelling on the Station Road."

The Station Road began at the Colborne Street (Lakeshore Road) corner, passing on the left in the first block the Wm. Whitaker & Sons complex of blacksmith shop, carriage works, or garage, depending upon the decade. A large residence (no.115) faced these buildings at the southeast corner of Church Street. This was the home of one of the sons and his family, William Whitaker Jr. (later William Whitaker Sr. upon his father's death). Jack and Walter were the other sons of Wm. Whitaker & Sons.

Close to the road on the northwest corner of Church Street stood the red-brick home of the Wilson family. Here, using the milk and cream from his father's "Gilbrae Farm" on Lakeshore Road West,

John W. Wilson's Gilbrae Dairy supplied dairy products to the households in town. A horse drawing one of the milk-wagons soon became familiar with the driver's route and, more often than not, stopped of its own accord at the homes of regular customers. The heavy glass milk-bottles, held upright in their wire-mesh carrier, were left at the door by the milkman according to the number of milk tickets left for him, or the instructions in a note; and a dollar might have been left for another strip of tickets (10 for $1.00). All this took place in the very early morning.

L.G. Snyder later operated the dairy, using the house for a dairy-bar and living in the former home of John Biggar next door on the north. The next two gabled homes were occupied by members of the Barrett family, and that on the Randall Street corner became the home and long-established plumbing business of George W. Barrett, father of Harry, our fine current Mayor.

Across Randall Street, in 1923 the Bell Telephone Company erected its new Exchange, contracted for and built by William H. Hawkes. Next door lived members of the Wass family and beside them Mrs. Wright-Orr, one of Oakville's busy piano teachers. The last house in that block was the home of Mr. and Mrs. Charles P. Chisholm (no.164). A large, grey frame-building, the Temperance Hall, had occupied the southeast corner of Randall Street since 1843 and had served a multitude of useful purposes, being once the headquarters of the Salvation Army. (After nearly 120 years, it was torn down and replaced by Tim Horton Donuts). The brick houses south of it in the block were constructed by Blakelock Brothers, builders and contractors.

Across Randall Street on the northeast corner stood the home of the Litchfield family (no.145), as attractive and well kept as it is today. A parking-lot north of the Litchfield home is all that remains of the ever-busy Carson and Sons Planing Mill, where the pleasant smell of freshly sawn lumber drifted out onto the Station Road. Later, when the Aluminum Company located on this site, the windows close to the sidewalk were well screened with wire mesh to prevent particles of aluminum from injuring passers-by. Mr. Alfred Conder, foreman at the Basket Factory, brought up his family of five fine children in his home (no.159) north of the planing mill just mentioned. The careful preservation of this home does credit to a member of the third generation living there at the present time.

The Station Road at Dunn Street was one of many pretty street corners in Oakville. An attractive home and garden at the southeast corner, with the park beyond, stood opposite the large residence (no.164) of Mr. Charles P. Chisholm, his garden on the corner surrounded by the same low, wrought-iron fence, set in concrete, which remains today. A deep perennial border bloomed all summer long just inside this fence and, among other lovely flowers there, I remember particularly the tall mauve heliotrope with the delicious perfume. (This corner lay on a route which I and many, many others took on foot several times a day. Those living in the north end of town used the short-cut through George's Square to Dunn Street when going to and from the downtown, and included pupils on their way to Central School on Navy Street and the High School on Reynolds. Dunn Street, then an ordinary two-way street, presented a very pretty view across the river to trees and open, undeveloped fields of grazing cattle on the opposite side. Lying along the south side of Dunn Street was the home (no.157) and large garden of Mr. W.H. Tuck, the town's prominent Funeral Director, Bandmaster, and fine citizen in general.)

George's Square,[3] usually spoken of simply as "the Park," was always a nice oasis in that part of town, especially while its tall white pines and other large trees were still standing. Because of its restful atmosphere, large bandstand for concerts, many benches, and iron pump for good drinking-water, the park was well used then by old and young. As well as the present diagonal path through the park, a similar path ran between the southeast and northwest corners, and was of great convenience to many people on foot. In 1921 the War Memorial was erected in George's Square, and on Armistice days everything came to a complete standstill throughout the town, while the citizens gathered at the park for a Service of Remembrance at the Cenotaph. Those unable to attend observed the two minutes of silence at 11:00 a.m. wherever they happened to be. For several years after the war public conveyances frequently came to a respectful two-minute stop at eleven o'clock on November 11.

On the northwest corner, between the edge of the creek bank and Dunn Street, Mr. Harry W. Page, brother of Dr. Charles Page, built a fine home. From that corner as far as Lawson Street, however, the west side of the pretty, curving Station Road was bare of houses. The street was indeed extremely attractive, with the deep ravine on the creek side, pleasant homes set in large gardens on the east, and beautiful overhanging trees on either side.

North of George's Square the first house on the east side (no.205) was the home in the 1800s and early 1900s of Dr. C.H.Lusk, who, as well as being a medical practitioner, was also briefly Assistant to the Principal in the old High School. He was a staunch Methodist, and the large addition to the Methodist Church in 1923 was named "Lusk

Hall" in his honour. For some time prior to the 1920s Mr. George W. Barrett occupied this home and added his plumbing shop to the east; the shop was later moved to Mr. Barrett's final location at Randall and Dundas streets. In the early 1920s no.205 was the home of Dr. Morley Wilkinson and his family, and the busy doctor served his devoted patients there for many long years.

Next on the north (no.217) lived the family of Mr. T.P. Thornton until they moved to Douglas Avenue at Belyea (MacDonald Road) in 1917. Mr. Ralph E. Young then purchased the house, which remained in the Young family until the 1960s. This home was a very familiar one to me, since I and a great number of my contemporaries spent our "teen" and later years enjoying ourselves there. The exterior has been altered by the removal of a particularly large, railed verandah along the west wall of the north section of the house.

Several families in turn occupied two brick houses in the middle of this block, and the Cordingly family lived on the southeast corner of what is now named Freestone Lane in recognition of Mr. John Freestone. Mr. Freestone lived on the northeast corner (no.235) and was a member of the family that at one time owned the Oakville Basket Factory. His property ran through to Reynolds, and two former Freeston homes still stand side by side on that street (nos. 207 and 213), just north of Palmer Avenue. In the early 1920s, no. 235 Dundas Street was the home of Mrs. Robinson (the former Faith Chisholm).

The Reverend J. E. Munro, minister of Knox Presbyterian Church from 1909 to 1925, lived with his family in "The Manse" (no.241). This house, which had been built in the late 1860s by John Potter, was bought a few years later by the Church to provide accommodation for its succeeding ministers. The Manse was always a pleasant sight then, set well back from the road in its large and pretty shady garden. In 1980 the Manse was moved forward to the road, covering the garden. To the north of it lived the Grice Family (no.247). It is said that in 1869, when the original house of Molly Menear near this site burned down, she built herself the nucleus of the present house by carrying the stone up the creek bank in her apron!

In the early 1920s Mr. and Mrs. Charles Johnston and their daughter Jessie, who formerly lived in the block below, moved to their attractive brick house (no.253), built shortly after the First World War. A pretty stucco house, since demolished, standing back from the street in its deeply shaded garden, was the home of Toronto lawyer Donald O. ("Doc") Cameron, who commuted for more years than most people could guess at. He was frequently consulted locally for his knowledge of gardening, his favourite hobby. Next door, in the present no.275, lived Mr. and Mrs. W.N. Kyle and son, Julian, who later made his home in the United States.

In 1911 Mr. and Mrs. J. T. Madden and daughter, Georgina, moved from the large C.W. Anderson home at Allan and Colborne streets (now Allan Street Apartments) to live on the Station Road (no.289). In the 1920s and later the Madden home was occupied by Mr. Lyman Root's family. Captain Francis J. Brown had built this house in the 1870s and his family had remained there for many years. Two or three acres of orchard lay north of no.289, between the Station Road and Reynolds Street, and on part of it, at Lawson Street, one of the first brick houses in Oakville, built by Samuel Lawson in 1837 and surrounded by apple trees, stood on a slight rise, facing the Station Road. This same house, considerably renovated, now faces on Lawson Street and is no.280. (When we lived here briefly in the early 1960s, two ancient apple trees from Mr. Lawson's original orchard still stood near the house.)

"Mariners' Home" (279 Lawson Street)

During 1900-30 the corner house north of Lawson Street faced the Station Road over a spacious lawn and garden, with shrubs and a white picket fence, and was the home of Mr. John Kelley, who was active in town affairs and served as a Mayor of Oakville. Built in the 1860s by Captain Robert Wilson and known later as "Mariners'

Home,"[4] it is now no.279 Lawson Street. An attractive bungalow on the creek bank (no.310) was bought by Mr. Sydney Furness, who lived there with his daughter Loys. This bungalow was the first building along the creek bank north of Dunn Street. Next along the river bank was the home of Mr. and Mrs. F. W. Meek and in the early 1920s the brothers T.A. and James Blakelock, contractors, built to the north of the Meek residence two fine brick houses side by side — the homes of Mr. R.E. Hore and Mr. Roy Smith, engineer for the county.

The site of the Basket Factory lay vacant for a number of years after the fire of 1920, but between Spruce Street and the Sixth Line (Old Mill Road) stood four houses on the creek bank, of which three had been built by the architect B.E.T. Ellis, one, in half-timbered style, for himself and his family. At the curve, where the Sixth Line turned off to the left following The Sixteen, stood the Robinson family's large frame-bungalow with its deep verandah and wide sloping lawns. At this intersection of the Sixth Line and Dundas Street[5] the residential part of the latter came to an end along the west side.

On the east side of Dundas Street, north of Lawson, lived Mr. and Mrs. Phillips Thompson and their son and daughter. Mr. Thompson, who had built this house (no.323) in 1912, was a writer for the *Globe* and commuted to Toronto every day. Their daughter became the mother of the famous Pierre Berton, while their son, Phillips Jr. ("Phil" or "P.W.T."), later made for himself a famous name in Oakville as an accomplished journalist and reporter of town events.

Phil wrote articles of general interest in the *Journal* and his regular weekly columns, such as "It Seems to Me" and "We Salute," in which he interviewed a great cross-section of townspeople, were written with deep feeling, understanding, and humour and were always read with interest. His valuable and informative column "Old Oakville," as well as other historical articles written for the *Journal* over a period of many years, contained a fund of information and was the result of endless research on his part and an on-going interest in anything to do with Oakville, past and present — an interest which remained with him until his death in 1973. (If this small tribute to Phil Thompson seems a digression from our time-span of 1900-30, it is because Phil's historical research and the recording of it in his newspaper columns, have been of value to so many hundreds of readers.)

The Galbraith family occupied no.331 Dundas Street, and in an impressive house (now nos. 337-39), standing in large grounds (nicknamed "Kerosene Kastle"[6]) lived Mr. W. S. Savage and his family. Members of the Ford family owned both no.349 and the home at the corner of Division Street (MacDonald Road).

"Kerosene Kastle" (337 Trafalgar Road)

Between Lawson Street and Division Street a slight incline began to be felt by those walking or riding up the Station Road, and in front of the Basket Factory, or later the ruins thereof, the steep slope tended to slow down pedestrians and horses, and later forced some of the very early motor cars to change gear! (The "Basket Factory hill" was eventually graded to a less noticeable slope.)

The Oakville Basket Factory is described in the chapter "Industries, 1900-1930." It was a factory of great importance and, until destroyed by fire in 1920, occupied the west side of the Station Road from Division Street (MacDonald Road) to Spruce Street, along the creek bank and on the slope of the so-called "hill." The company office was located across the street, at the northeast corner of Division Street. After the fire, the Basket Factory moved to a new location south of the Oakville Station.

Halfway up the east side of the Basket Factory hill (no.373) lived the family of Mr. Hannah, on the southeast corner of Spruce that of Mr. W.T. Merry, and across Spruce Street (no.397) the family of Mr. Charles F. Doty, head of the large lumber company Davis and Doty Limited (now the Beaver Lumber Company). Next was the home (no.407) of Mr. W.A. Inglehart, who in those years owned a part of the former Chisholm farm in that area. In 1909 the "Inglehart Survey" was responsible for the development of the land in the north end of town between Dundas and Reynolds and the opening up of Inglehart Avenue between the two streets.

Mr. Lorne C. Ashbury, one of the sons of T.H. Ashbury and Sons lived (no.423) near the point at which the Sixth Line (Old Mill Road) proceeded a short distance to the steep hill which led down the creek bank to Mr. Ashbury's place of business at the grist mill. Mr. Herbert A. Ashbury, his brother, and family lived in pretty, shady grounds at the top of this "Mill hill." (The spacious and once most attractive Herbert Ashbury home is barely visible now, wedged in between the headquarters of the Halton Regional Police—District 2 and the King Paving Company, but, having found it, you will be repaid by a lovely view from high above The Sixteen across to the opposite bank.)

On the east side of Dundas Street, near the curve at the Sixth Line, a large, red-brick house stood on shaded lawns, the home of Mr. Robert Menzie and his family (now the Esso Station, *et al.*). To the north lay orchards and gardens as far as the intersection with Inglehart Avenue. At the end of the First World War Mr. Frederick Harris came from England and built here his large publishing house, the Frederick Harris Music Company (no.461); in 1922 a red-brick building arose where Dundas and Inglehart Avenue met and housed a branch of the Royal Bank of Canada (Mr. I. N. Tompkins, manager).

Before one turned left to the Oakville Station, it was worthwhile following Reynolds for a short distance along the north side, to its turn southward at Pine Avenue. On the corner stood a delightfully proportioned, one-storey home. (no.453) of white stucco and green trim, complete with verandahs with their original trim on the west and south sides. Many years before, the nucleus of this house, which had stood on original Crown Land acquired by William Chisholm in 1831, had been moved a short distance to this location, remaining as part of the John A. Chisholm Sr. family farm until the late 1800s. There is in existence a photograph showing members of the Chisholm family grouped on the front verandah of this home, including little Hazel[8] at her grandmother's knee. From 1910 Mr. and Mrs. Chamberlain raised a fine family of future citizens of Oakville here. This historic home was immaculately cared for and enhanced the corner for the 70 years it was occupied by the Chamberlain family. Tragically, it was demolished in 1981.

Returning to Dundas Street, one turned left into the approach to the Oakville Station,[9] which was situated on the south side of the railway tracks. Most Railway Stations along the line boasted a nearby hotel for the convenience of commercial travellers, and Oakville was no exception, for here, sure enough, was George Haynes' Railway

John Chisholm Sr. Farm House (mid-1800s)
(1910-80, home of Chamberlain family. Demolished 1981)

Hotel — tall, narrow, and slightly wedge-shaped. Although it was a small building, the ground floor was a lively spot at train time, and well patronized for morning or evening newspapers, magazines, cigars, cigarettes, and snacks. I never remember hearing anything said concerning accommodation at the Railway Hotel but I do recall that George Haynes was a great favourite with commuters, and knew enough to save a favourite brand of cigar for a steady customer or two. Arthur Tuck, in his grocery store at the intersection of Reynolds and Inglehart Avenue (no.491 Inglehart), also enjoyed a faithful following of commuters, who would drop in for a quick purchase there before the final dash for the train, standing panting at the Station.

Beyond this point, Dundas Street led to the level crossing over the railway tracks, protected by man-controlled gates. The gateman we were all most familiar with was "Dad" Redshaw, who was stationed in a glass-sided look-out shelter at the north side of the tracks and who, before lowering the gates, would sound a bell of warning (occasionally, an extra bell of greeting!). A lighted lantern was hung after dark on each of the double gates on both sides of the tracks and, to my knowledge, no accident occurred at this particular level crossing.

Dundas Street continued to the town limit where, after crossing the Lower Middle Road, it became the Seventh Line, running north through the County of Halton.

Footnotes:

[1] The Post family owned much property along what is now Highway no.5, from the Ninth to the Sixth Line (Munn's Corners). The junction of the Seventh Line was known first as Post's Corners, when Ephraim Post opened his tavern and stage-coach inn here early in the 1800s (enlarged by son Hiram in 1841). The name later became Postville. Many, many members of the Post family lived until recent years at the Corners and in the vicinity. The Post family also owned large grants of land in early York (Toronto), and Jordan and Melinda streets in downtown Toronto were named by Jordan Post for himself and his wife. At some time in the later 1900s Postville was renamed Trafalgar; the village has since disappeared.
[2] Red Hill: the shore cliff of Lake Ontario's predecessor, Lake Iroquois.
[3] George's Square: named by William Chisholm for his father and marked on the map of Oakville of 1835.
[4] Captain Robert Wilson's home, built in 1862, was known later as "Mariners' Home" because of his custom of giving a home to ill and homeless sailors during the winters. Captain Wilson was loved also by many black people whom he had helped to escape slavery during the Civil War, giving them space as stowaways in his grain vessels returning from the United States.
[5] In the early 1800s this junction was the location of a toll-gate operated by Mr. Donald Campbell, toll-keeper. (Mr. Campbell's home, one of the few brick houses in Oakville at that time, stands restored, at the northwest corner of Reynolds Street and MacDonald Road.)
[6] This house of interesting architecture was built by Mr. R. S. Wood in 1856 across the road from his Oakville Oil Refinery, where kerosene, or coal-oil, was refined in large quantities. For this reason, the large house was nicknamed "Kerosene Kastle." Unfortunately, fire destroyed the refinery in 1866 and Mr. Wood then lived for some years in no.85 Navy Street.
[7] What is left of the "Mill-hill road" appears as nothing more than a pathway now; it can be seen by those driving downhill from Kerr Street over the "Third Crossing."
[8] Hazel (Chisholm) Mathews
[9] Mr. W.B. Shipley was stationmaster during the 1920s and 1930s.

Central School (built 1850s, demolished 1960s)

6
Educating the Young

THE OAKVILLE PUBLIC SCHOOL

The Oakville Public School (Central School), which was built in 1850, was beginning to show signs of wear and tear by the 1900s. Nevertheless, no school building could have been better designed as far as such things as safety and good lighting were concerned. Each and every school-room had large windows on both sides, giving natural lighting all day long. Each and every school-room had two accesses as well, one door leading to the inner halls of the building and the other, at the opposite end of the room, opening to the outside. The outside doors from the second-floor rooms led to a wide, enclosed staircase, while those on the ground floor opened directly outside. There would be little use in pretending that the sanitary facilities were of the first order — such things had not yet been perfected in 1850. However, the building was comfortably warm, heated by hot-water (or steam?) heating using soft coal; the rooms were kept clean and the floors oiled regularly. Above all, *education* was going on here of the highest calibre.

Basics were doggedly implanted in one's young brain by very dedicated teachers, and each pupil had little choice but to absorb it all. Hundreds would agree with me that pupils who were prepared for the High School Entrance Examinations (Grade VIII) by Principal R. F. Sanderson still retain most of what "Sandy" taught them during that year! Sandy's teaching was of a design to last and fortunately his teaching years were many, so that a host of boys and girls had the advantage (though some were not inclined, at the time, to recognize it as such!) of passing through the hands of an exceptionally gifted teacher.

BRANTWOOD SCHOOL, 1921 and WESTWOOD SCHOOL, 1923

By 1920 the population of Oakville had begun to increase rather rapidly, and as a result the downtown Central School became overcrowded. Since most of the new houses were being constructed in the "Brantwood Survey" and surrounding areas, it was decided to build a new school on Allan Street, which would accommodate the junior classes and thus relieve the pressure on Central School. Since the new school was located within the limits of the survey, it was naturally named Brantwood School. As the town continued to grow, a new public school, Westwood, was opened in 1923 at Rebecca and Wilson streets on the west side of the river. Both Westwood and Brantwood were included, understandably, within the Oakville Public School System.

ST. MARY'S SEPARATE SCHOOL, 1860

During many years of the 1900s the boys and girls of St. Mary's Roman Catholic School were lucky enough to benefit from the exceptional teaching of Miss Mary McDermott; her pupils remained with her during all their school years until they entered High School. The school was located east of St. Andrew's Roman Catholic Church on King Street. In the same location today, it is now École Ste. Marie.

MAPLE GROVE SCHOOL, 1872

Maple Grove School has always stood, from its earliest beginnings, on the Ninth Line (Maplegrove Road), of Trafalgar Township. It was, therefore, known to all as "the Ninth Line School." Serving the section of the township east of Oakville, it enjoyed a reputation for excellent teaching and good discipline. A one-room school until the 1930s, when a second room plus a basement and hot-water heating were added, it was then renamed Maple Grove for the large maple trees which lined the school-yard.

PINE GROVE SCHOOL, 1872

Pine Grove School performed the same service for the pupils living in the Township of Trafalgar west of Oakville. It was situated on the Fourth Line but is now barely visible as no.607 Stephen Crescent. Pine Grove School was a landmark in 1900—30, surrounded by a beautiful stand of white pine.

The Ontario Department of Education placed a great deal of emphasis at the public school level on learning about our own country. The capitals, principal rivers, lakes, and physical features of each province were fixed in our minds by the free-hand drawing of map after map of Canada showing their positions. The industries and products of each province were studied as well. Teaching methods were reinforced by a good deal of oral repetition. The capital city, principal rivers, and general position of all other countries in the world were also learned by the map-drawing method. In the case of our own province, most pupils could soon draw, almost with eyes closed, a free-hand map of the Great Lakes and river systems. We learned by rote the counties and county towns of Ontario in relation to their location: those around each of the Great Lakes; those situated inland; and those along the St. Lawrence and Ottawa rivers. I, myself, have found all the above extremely useful information to have firmly fixed in my head as I've travelled around the country over many years.

The method of studying poetry and the classics in earlier days was a thorough examination and explanation of the piece, followed by memorization of it. Although I am fully aware that this method of teaching is frowned upon today, it was then used throughout the schools, both public and private. One result is that I can still recall from memory, after 60 years or more, a great store of lovely extracts, complete with their context. Later, in High School, whole passages were memorized from Shakespeare and the classic poets and, when we were exposed to "Scripture lessons," many passages from the Bible as well. Contrary to modern belief, once learned these words and meanings remain as a "reserve" throughout one's lifetime. I do not pretend that everything learned by memory is retained, but only that, when met with again later, it is familiar enough to be more easily comprehended and enjoyed. Multiplication tables and rules learned by rote were automatically remembered, and proved useful in the study of mathematical subjects.

THE OAKVILLE HIGH SCHOOL

Until 1910 the Oakville High School occupied rooms facing Navy

Oakville High School, 1915

Street in the old Oakville Public School building; a new school was then built on Reynolds Street in its present location. Mr. J. T. Lillie, who had pressed the need for larger accomodation, was Principal at both the old and the new High School locations. Shortly before the First World War Mr. W. B. Weidenhammer became Principal, and during the war years he changed his surname to "Wyndham." At first nicknamed "Weidy," and then for many years affectionately known as "Wyndy." he was always the perfect gentleman, quiet and unobtrusive. He was, nevertheless, "everywhere at once" and maintained a tight control over the whole school.

The academic standard of O.H.S. was rated high, as was the school spirit. Sports were entered into with great enthusiasm and frequent Rugby and hockey matches, played against rival school teams, were always accompanied by a full turn-out of boys and girls, shouting and screaming respectively!

On Friday afternoons after school the Literary Society held its meetings in the large Assembly Hall. These meetings were a great outlet for any talents the students might possess; such activities as debating, musical recitals, glee club, and dramatics took place, and a good deal of after-school practising and rehearsing was undertaken for these events. Concerts were held in the evenings, and when, after a few years, the one or two members of the Board of Education who held out against it (and who shall remain nameless!) were persuaded to relent, dancing was finally allowed in the Assembly Hall, to the delight of all. A large addition to the High School was completed in January 1924.

Early during the First World War Mr. Wyndham, who was extremely public-spirited, agreed to help the war effort in the summer by seeing to the tending of a large field of beans, which had been planted north of the High School playing-fields. (Whether this was a town or a High School project I never knew — or cared!) As the summer term drew to a close Mr. Wyndham asked among the students for volunteer "farmerettes" and what happened to the hundreds of other students I never knew, but when school closed the number of volunteers had boiled down to two — my great friend Margaret Turner and myself.

The Oakville Hospital complex now covers what was then a grassy field sloping gently from the High School up to Division Street (MacDonald Road). The eastern portion of this field along Allan Street had become overnight (or so it seemed) a vast field of beans: row after row of plants and weeds struggling up through what we knew in that section of Oakville as "blow-sand." Well, a promise was a promise, so we arrived for duty each morning — dressed appropriately in long khaki overalls, topped off with a large "cow's breakfast" straw hat. Mr. Wyndham was kindness and sympathy itself, bringing us cold drinks (he lived across from the High School in what is now no.297 Allan Street) and often picking up another hoe and working along with us. I don't remember how long we kept up this nightmare, but I'm certain that we did not last to harvest the crop! I vowed then that if there were ever another war, I would not again do my duty as a "farmerette."

Mr. Wyndham was followed as Principal by Mr. R. H. Archibald, who also guided the teachers and students of O.H.S. successfully for many years.

THE I.O.F. ORPHANS' HOME

In the early 1900s the international fraternal society the Independent Order of Foresters chose Oakville as the location for a home (no.53 Bond Street) for the orphaned children of deceased members. These children came from across Canada, the United States, and elsewhere, and were happy at the home, well cared for and well supervised by Mr. J. C. Morgan, an outstanding administrator and superintendent. In their turn, Mr. J. W. West and Mr. A.G. Holmstead devoted themselves to the welfare of the boys and girls under their care.

The I.O.F Orphans' Home was set in several acres of farmland and orchards, and part of the children's education lay in learning something of agriculture by helping to tend the farm produce grown on the property. The children went to the Oakville Public School and, receiving good supervision at the Home, did well in their studies. Each Sunday they walked across the Radial Bridge to attend Morning Service and afternoon Sunday school at St. Jude's Church and were a credit to the good care they received at the Home. This handsome building on Bond Street, standing at the head of Wilson Street, was used as Ortona Barracks during the Second World War and is now incorporated in the Oaklands Regional Centre for the Retarded.

KINDERGARTEN AND SCHOOLS FOR THE YOUNG

Mrs. Dorothy (Chisholm) Souter gives us here some recollection of her first days in the sphere of "education."

"Miss Violet and Miss Kathleen Appelbe opened a kindergarten and music school, which both my sister Ruth and I attended, in their home on the southeast corner of Navy and King streets. In a year or two, however, "Miss Violet" married Mr. Twigg and went to live in Vancouver. I remember the wedding reception held in their garden, and the tremendous hats and long trailing dresses worn by the ladies. Miss Kathleen Appelbe became one of the foremost piano teachers in Oakville for an unknown number of years.

"My sister Ruth and I next attended the school of Mrs. Sheldrake and Miss Shaw. Their house still stands on the southeast corner of King and Reynolds streets. Mrs. Sheldrake taught the junior children, who included a few small boys, but I think these were 'thinned out' before they moved on to Miss Shaw's class of older children. We learned French from *French Without Tears* — an excellent little text-book used in all junior schools where French was taught at that time. In spite of its title, many of the stories ended instead on quite a tearful note.

"Mrs. Sheldrake's brings back memories of a strong smell of 'banana oil' which we mixed with 'gold' powder to paint many valentines, and Christmas, St. Patrick's Day, and Easter cards. We spent a good deal of time turning these out. We began learning here our first multiplication tables, and were taught sewing and a few little songs.

Outdoors, we played hopscotch, skipped rope on the sidewalks, and enjoyed many other games that were popular at the time.

"The next private school we attended was presided over by Miss Willis, assisted by her aunt, Miss Boulton. This school was upstairs in Mr. Davis' building (nos.185—89 Lakeshore East), over Byers' Drug Store and across the hall from my father's law office. We were here only briefly, however, before we were sent to join our brothers in the Public School"

I attended Miss Willis' School for a few years longer than Dorothy, and following that Miss Vera Crossley's School in the same location. The ladies mentioned above were all good teachers, and we learned the rudiments of reading, spelling, arithmetic, geography, poetry, and art. Subsequently, Miss Creighton opened a school in her home no.50 Second Street. Dorothy Souter continues:

"Mrs. Sheldrake held dancing classes during the Winter in the large Anderson's Hall on "the Main Street" (nos. 134-38 Lakeshore East). While Miss Shaw played the piano, we learned the waltz and two step, as well as 'Sir Roger de Coverley,' the schottische, and other dances."

These dancing classes were "mixed" and we were taught, among many other points of etiquette, how to respond properly to a boy inviting you to have the next dance, who was supposed to say, "May I have the pleasure?" More difficult was knowing how to go about trying to keep in step with one's partner — *one*-two-three; *one*-two-three" — this was sometimes rather trying!

MISS LIGHTBOURN'S SCHOOL, 1923

The famous private school of Miss Ruth Lightbourn, whose name is perpetuated today in St. Mildred's Lightbourn School (no.1080 Linbrook Road), began in 1923 in a very small way. The headmaster of Appleby School, Mr. J.S.H. Guest, had a problem. Although he had secured the best teachers he could find to provide an education for the nearly 100 boys in his care, he was at a loss to know how or where to secure an education for his two small daughters, Betty and Kitty. Since a school full of boys did not seem to Mr. Guest an ideal setting for their education, he approached Miss Ruth Lightbourn, asking her if she would undertake to teach them. This Ruth agreed to do, and the girls were brought each school day to the Lightbourn home on Dunn Street (no.31).

But Ruth Lightbourn was an exceptionally gifted teacher, and in no time the word spread to other parents in Oakville, who clamoured to have their children taught by her also. Soon the number of students, including a few small boys, increased to fill two of the downstairs rooms of the Lightbourn home, and in 1929 Ruth moved her school to a house on the east side of Park Avenue (no.65). Very soon the effects of the Depression were felt and the school moved to smaller quarters on Dundas Street (no.235 Trafalgar Road). As the Depression years eased, enrolment increased again and the school moved in 1937 to its site for so many years at no.220 Reynolds Street. (In 1940 an "overflow" nursery school was held in Victoria Hall, directly across the street.) Miss Lightbourn's School continued until her retirement in 1958, and many, many of her loyal graduates are spread far and wide.

Sports Day, 1920s

APPLEBY SCHOOL, 1911

This boarding-school for boys,[1] founded by Sir Edmund Walker of Toronto with his son-in-law, John S. H. Guest, as headmaster, opened its doors on September 14, 1911, to its first "Appleby boys" — 28 in number. The property, two miles west of Oakville, chosen in 1909 for the school had once been part of the original farm of the McCraney family, and was then owned by Judge Colin G. Snider of Hamilton, who agreed to sell to his friend, Sir Edmund, the acreage he required for the buildings and grounds of the new school.

Even before construction of the large, red-brick "School House," which was to mean "Appleby" to so many hundreds of boys and men of the future, Mr. Guest's ceaseless energy and foresight were at work planning the essential playing-fields and over-all detail connected with the school of his dreams. One of his priorities was the diversion of McCraney's Creek, whose natural course ran through the middle of the lower field, already envisaged by Mr. Guest as the school's future cricket pitch and playing-fields. He had the course of the creek diverted to run close to the west bank or boundary of the school property, creating for the future not only, indeed, an unsurpassed

"School House", c.1912

cricket, Rugby, and soccer field, but a natural amphitheatre for the Annual Sports, Prize-giving, Cadet Corps Inspections, and other functions.

Appleby was named for the ancient Grammar School of Appleby Magna, in Leicestershire, England, which Mr. Guest and his ancestors had attended as boys. Said to have been designed by Sir Christopher Wren, it had closed its doors in the 1800s, and it seemed appropriate to

Mr. Guest to adopt its name for his new school in Canada, which would follow the traditions of its namesake as an English Public School, complete with the prefect system and strict attention to discipline.

The school building (or School House; later Colley House[2]) was well designed to contain classrooms, accommodation for some 40 boys, and all the many facilities necessary to their daily well-being. The housemaster, his assistant, and the female household staff were accommodated here; under the same roof also were the dining-rooms, kitchen, locker-rooms billiard-room, and the headmaster's and secretary's[3] offices. Not least in importance was the coal-furnace in the basement, alongside the large coal-bins, which were kept filled by Hillmer's Fuel & Ice Company and tended faithfully by John Emery, to name only one. Outlying buildings of wood-shingle near School House contained the science lab, the school hospital and nurse's quarters, and the tuck-shop; there were also bungalows for masters' families and the male employees. The headmaster's large, stone house stood overlooking the lake.

In 1913 an ancient barn (near the site of the present Chapel) was completely destroyed by a disastrous fire, in which the school lost horses and equipment as well as a number of ponies belonging to the boys. It was immediately replaced by the barn which still stands close to the Lakeshore Road. Work-horses and farm equipment were essential for the groundsmen[4] who endlessly tended the playing-fields and beautified the rolling, grassy slopes between highway and lake. These men were busy in Winter with general maintenance, not only coping with snow on roadways and walkways but "making ice" on the large and small outdoor rinks (and later in the 1920s in the covered rink).

When Appleby's second year brought an unforeseen increase in enrolment, the McCraney farm on the north side of the highway was leased and the old McCraney house fitted up as well as possible for a master (Mr. V.H. de B. Powell), a housekeeper, and 13 boys. This was the original Powell's House, and was replaced only in 1918 by the venerable Powell's House of today. The old residence continued to provide accommodation for a small number of boys and master-in-charge. It was given the pseudonym "New House"! Good use was made of the McCraney farmland between the highway and the Radial Car tracks (now Rebecca Street), and the school was almost self-sustaining in the early years, as far as garden produce was concerned.

In 1919 the nucleus of the beautiful, stone Memorial Chapel was built; completed in 1929 it is now enlarged and known as the John Bell

Chapel. Boarders and day-boys alike attended their own Chapel service each morning before classes, and on Sunday mornings the boarders walked to St. Jude's, Knox Presbyterian, or St. Andrew's churches. They were then free to accept invitations to visit day-boys' families, or other friends, until their Chapel hour at 7:00 p.m. Appleby boys were a welcome addition to the town as far as Oakville girls were concerned: the influx of so many extra boys was a dream come true, and suspense built up while the girls awaited an invitation to the annual Appleby "Formal," held just before the Christmas holidays. For the boys this meant instruction in the latest dance-steps, and a crash course in the niceties of escorting a young lady to a formal affair!

The grass tennis-courts and "manicured" cricket pitch were kept in faultless condition through the assistance and interest of one of Appleby's first, and most notable, masters. Distinguished as the school's science master, Mr. E. W. Whittington possessed the proverbial green thumb and was never happier than when tending his flowers, growing vegetables, and mowing tennis-courts, etc., with his hand-mower. It would not surprise me if some of his lovely bulbs still bloom each Spring along the west bank, beyond the creek!

A graduate of Caius (pronounced kees) College, Cambridge, and experienced as headmaster of the Lower School at Upper Canada College, Mr. Guest had exceptional talents as teacher, administrator, and disciplinarian (in the fairest sense of the word), and his influence was felt everywhere throughout Appleby. Besides being himself an outstanding teacher, he possessed a knack for choosing other masters of a high calibre and, since classes were small the boys received an excellent education. It was well-rounded education as well, with a heavy accent on sports, in which each boy in the school was expected to participate. In addition to the usual Rugby, soccer, hockey, and cricket there were boxing and gymnastics as well as dramatics and training in the Cadet Corps and the Bugle Band. It all added up to a well-occupied schoolboy. In short, Appleby School (later Appleby College) proudly turned out boys who were educated to take their place in society, and many an Appleby Old Boy has made a name for himself in the world at large.

Footnotes:

[1] The name Appleby School was changed to Appleby College on March 5, 1941.
[2] Colley House: named in honour of Thomas B. Colley, its revered housemaster for 35 years (1914-49), which included his years of service in the First World War.
[3] By great good fortune I was secretary to Mr. Guest for six years before his retirement in 1934, and later, intermittently for 11 years, to the Reverend John Bell, D.D.
[4] Notably, George Adams and James McMillan, dedicated workers during Appleby's first decade and longer.

7
Lakeshore Road & Colborne Street (south side)

"The Lakeshore" between Toronto and Hamilton was a pretty road, heavily lined with trees. A dirt road until the First World War years, when it was paved with cement, it still remained a two-lane highway, known as Lakeshore, or no.2, Highway. Even before its paving a general influx of "people of means" had been taking place along the lakefront, both east and west of the Ninth Line (Maplegrove Road), where large acreages of property were being purchased and built upon by prosperous businessmen from Toronto, Hamilton, and elsewhere.

Among the the residents east of the Ninth Line, on the south side, were Dr. Scadding, Mr. J.J. Vaughan, Mrs. E.B. Holcroft, Mr. W. Stone, and Mr. Ryland H. New. Immediately to the east of the Ninth Line Mr. J.J. Follett of Toronto built a handsome house on the lake (no.2024), which was the home until recently of the family and descendants of Mr. Cyrus A. Birge of Hamilton. In 1909 Mr. James Ryrie, a Toronto jeweller, bought a large acreage north of the Lakeshore Road, as well as the land opposite along the lakefront to the west of Mr. Follett's; there he built his home and landscaped his lovely estate "Edgemere" (no.1502). Farther to the west, Mr. Herbert C. Cox of the Canada Life Assurance Company of Toronto bought around the same time a property of 17 acres, named the estate "Ennisclare," and soon completed his handsome and spacious home near the lake, (no.40 Cox Drive). Great stables, other buildings, and an arena stood near Lakeshore Road to accommodate his famous thoroughbred horses, some of the finest hunters and jumpers in North America. These animals, many of which were imported from Ireland and elsewhere, were trained under the direction of an expert in horsemanship, Mr. "Hughie" Wilson,[1] who won prizes both for his own and for the Ennisclare stables, far and wide.

From Mr. Cox's fine stable of horses was formed the famous Ennisclare Hunt, which had its beginnings in the years 1910-12. An excellent pack was made up of fine breeds of dogs secured from other parts of Canada and from the United States. Not content with the local foxes, the Hunt brought in a better breed from Prince Edward Island, whose chief, and very successful, industry at that time was fox-farming. West of the stables was a large polo field,[2] internationally known as one of the finest. Polo became a very popular sport and many of the best teams played there. A number of Oakville riders owned their own mounts and enjoyed thoroughly both the polo and the Hunt.

The entire Cox property along the Lakeshore Road was bordered by a rough-cast wall some six feet in height. A short section of this wall still remains on the north side of the road, as well as a longer one on the south. During the First World War Mr. Cox set aside a large part of his land for growing fruits and vegetables in aid of the war effort. He provided, as well, living-quarters and transportation for some dozen or so "farmerettes" and others who worked hard during the war years to help ensure sufficient food for Canada and for the Canadian troops.

West of Ennisclare, in 1923—24, Colonel W. G. MacKendrick built his fine home[3] on the lakefront at the mouth of Coates' Creek (now Morrison Creek). On the roadway leading from Lakeshore Road to his home, Colonel MacKendrick later gave space for homes for two of his married children. In 1960 the MacKendrick house and property were bought by James Gairdner, who later bequeathed them to the Town of Oakville as "Gairloch Gardens."

In the early 1900s, when travelling on the Lakeshore, we used to cross a rather noisy bridge of loose planks over Coates' Creek, which had been named after the father and son through whose farm it ran and who operated a large and successful sawmill on it (those being the days before the water in the creek became a mere trickle). When the old wooden St. Jude's Church of England still stood on the northwest corner of Colborne and Thomas streets, Richard Coates, who was both musical and a skilled craftsman, built its first organ from wood processed in the mill on his creek. On the other side of Coates' Creek Mr. W. H. Brouse and his family lived in their large, two-storey, rough-cast home (no.1248), built about 1906. The house stood close to Lakeshore Road, enclosed by a wooden fence and hedge, and the property, which reached down to the lake, was planted with orchards and gardens. Later, this became the home of Mr. James. A. Gairdner and his family.

After living for a few years on the Eaton property farther west on Lakeshore Road (no.452), Mr. W.F. Eaton acquired property next to Mr. Brouse and on it built a sizeable stone house set in the middle of picturesque gardens, naming the estate "Ballymena" (no.1208). Stable, garage, and gardener's quarters stood to the left of the centre gates. Mr. and Mrs. Eaton were most generous about opening their grounds and home for the benefit of worthy causes, and their kindness was always much appreciated. (In recent years, this house was occupied by the Honourable Ray and Mrs. Lawson.) Earlier, around 1907, Mr. F.A. Prime from Toronto had built a large, half-timbered home halfway between the road and the lake. A handsome gateway stood at the entrance and the house (no.1176) was reached by a fine avenue of trees. Mr. Prime was prominent in helping to organize the Oakville Club and became President near the beginning of its formation. He possessed a fine tenor voice, and a bronze memorial tablet near the choir stalls in St. Jude's Church bears record of the fact that he sang in the choir there for many years.

Mr. William Molesworth brought his family from Toronto to a newly built, three-storey home on his property immediately west of Mr. Prime's. This attractive, brown-shingled house (no.1150) was designed by Mr. Molesworth's architect son, George N. Molesworth, who was responsible for many fine houses in Oakville. The house faced east and was slightly elevated on a small, nicely landscaped terrace on property which reached down to the lake. Near the lake, Mr. Molesworth built a cottage for use during the summer. A short distance west was a large, white, somewhat older home (no.1118), occupied in the early 1900s by Dr. Port and his family. One of his sons, Nelson, was a great friend of my brother Philip, then in his teens. It interests me now to recall that Philip and his friend attended St. Andrew's School in Toronto (not at that time in Aurora), as far as I remember, as day-boys. How on earth did we all cover the ground!

A dense "bush" separated Dr. Port's property from "The Grove," the home of Mrs. F. W. Phillips and her son and daughter, Alec and Dorothy. Mrs. Phillips' father, Mr. Alexander Robertson from Stirling, Scotland, had acquired 35 acres from the estate of Judge Beardsley, known as "Beardsley's Grove." In the 1850s he proceeded to put teams of oxen to work to clear space for his house and buildings, and for the cultivation of apple and pear orchards and other fruit, especially strawberries, leaving a wide section of his property on the east heavily wooded. The fine wood used throughout the house (no.76

Alexander Drive) in its stair-rails, door, and panelling came from trees on this land, sawn in a local mill. My mother was a great friend of Mrs. Phillips, and I of Dorothy and Alec, and the magic of those beautiful woods (carpeted with the wild hepatica, trillium, columbine, violet, and Solomon's seal) and the memories of their lovely garden, the picnics, and bathing in the lake at the bottom of their orchards are not easily forgotten. Although the lovely old homestead is nearly obscured by surrounding houses now, a beautiful survivor, a sturdy copper beech, still stands proudly where Mr. Robertson planted it so many years ago as a seedling brought out from Scotland. This tree stood inside the north fence of his pretty shaded garden. Other survivors still grow near the Phillips family's home.

When we lived 'down the shore' the Beardsley residence (no.1028), the next house west of Mrs. Phillips', was occupied by a Dr. Patterson, the only veterinarian, I believe, in Oakville. Early in the First World War, however, Mr. W. D. Gregory sold his newly built home and estate farther west and moved with his family to the Beardsley property, which ran along the Eighth Line (Chartwell Road) south to the lake; they were to live there for many years. While overseas during the war Mr. Gregory's son, Goldwin, met and married an attractive Belgian girl. On their return to Canada Mr. Gregory built a new home (no.1014), just west of his own, for Goldwin and his "Belgian Bride"! W. D. Gregory and Goldwin were partners in the law firm of Gregory and Gregory in Toronto.

In the first decade of the 1900s the Sutherland family lived at the southwest corner of the Eighth Line and Lakeshore Road. Their house, which faced the highway, was surrounded by a beautifully kept, high cedar hedge, and a hedge-lined path led to the front verandah. During the war years this became the home of Mr. and Mrs. Charles Cox and their daughter Dorothy. The cedar hedge secluded the gardens from the traffic on Lakeshore Road and Mr. Cox, a tennis enthusiast, laid out an excellent grass tennis-court on the lawn slightly northeast of the house. His enthusiasm caught on quickly with his own generation, and spread like wild-fire among Dorothy's friends. Very many happy hours were enjoyed there by us all. Although still standing, this home (no.92 Chartwell) is no longer located on Lakeshore Road, since its gardens, tennis-court, hedges, and trees have been replaced by houses.

From 1905 to 1906 Howard and Park avenues were being busily built up by contractors Carson and Bacon, but I do not recall houses between those avenues on Lakeshore Road until the 1920s. A vacant field at the southwest corner of Park Avenue ended at a long grey-stone wall, in the centre of which was a wide wooden gate. From it a curved driveway, with lawn, trees, and flower-beds on either side, led to "Montacute House," Mr. W. D. Gregory's spacious stone residence (no. 452) built in 1909 close to the lake and not visible from Lakeshore Road. Jean was the youngest of this family, and she and I, and others of the same age, found it a wonderful place to play. Jean, who was quite a "horse person" even then, possessed a square wicker pony-cart, with seats on three sides, drawn by a very gentle Shetland pony: this was considered safe for all ages! Many picnics and parties were held there for us as children, as well as for Mr. and Mrs. Gregory's friends, and memories of the Gregory family are happy ones.

Mr. A. B. Gordon bought this beautiful property from Mr. Gregory at some time during the First World War, naming it "Raymar" after his two daughters, Ray and Marjorie. Later, it became the estate of Mrs. Timothy Eaton and was subsequently occupied by the families of Mr. and Mrs. Burden and Mr. and Mrs. W.F. Eaton. The property (no.452) still retains the name Raymar.

Lakeshore Road had become Colborne Street a short distance before reaching Second Street, where a pleasant two-storey house[5] with verandah stood at the southeast corner (no.93 Second). Shaded by apple trees, it had a picket fence on two sides, with a corner gate. This was the home of Mr. and Mrs. Harry Taylor and their daughter and son, Victoria and Banfield. At some time in the 1920s it became the home of the accomplished artists Mr. Caleb Keene and his wife, Minna, and their brilliant son and daughter, Louis and Violet. Many and beautiful works of art were done in this house and studio in their time.

Second Street, I knew with my eyes shut. During "my youth" my mother's first cousin Mabel Sydney lived in no.74 with four delightful and vivacious daughters, Madge, Lilian, Dudley, and Eleanor, and as much time was spent there as in my own home on Gloucester Avenue. My contemporary, Eleanor, and I left no stone unturned in the neighbourhood, no fence or tree unclimbed; we knew as much of our neighbours' business as was possible, and our summers were spent with others at the lake at the foot of the street. We read endless books together and, when that palled, set off to discover new worlds on roller-skates or bicycle.

The present no.75 had been in the very early 1900s the home of Dr. Black, and was owned later by the W.D. Gregory family, whose property adjoined on the east. The Arnoldi family of Toronto next acquired the property, family members, the Warrens, living there during the war time. For many years this was the home of Mr. and Mrs. Ross Ostrom, Gil, and Curzon. Several tenants occupied no.69 until it became the home of Mr. and Mrs. Ernest F. Pullen. (Mr. Pullen's brother Frank's home, "Old Orchard" (no.135 Watson Avenue), was the first to be built north of Colborne Street — at which point the name Second Street changed to Watson Avenue. Here lived Gwyneth, Hugh, Ernest, Nanette, and Tom.) Below the Ernest Pullen property on Second Street ran a secondary entrance to Raymar, and south of this driveway stood the substantial home (no.51) of Charles ("Chum") Green, Mrs. Green, Laura, and Bremner. During a large part of 1900-30 an apple orchard filled most of the space down to the home of Mr. and Mrs. T. R. Jarvis, who lived overlooking the lake at the end of the street.

Open property along the lake front and on the west side of Second Street belonged to Mr. W.G. Jaffray, whose own home stood on First Street. A cottage (demolished in the late 1970s) was in earlier days occupied by Mr. Lewis, chauffeur to Mr. Jaffray. In the two brick houses to the north (nos.50 and 56) lived Mr. and Mrs. D.D. How and the family of Joseph Lyon, an intrepid member of the Volunteer Fire Brigade. The north corner of Union Street was the home of R.F. Sanderson, Principal of Oakville Central School, and in no. 70 lived Mr. J.B.L. Grout, Manager of the Bank of Toronto, Mr. and Mrs. Grout being the parents of Helen and Bob. The latter dear little tow-headed boy was, from a very early age, constantly being asked his name, for the simple pleasure of hearing his patient, polite, and invariable answer: "My name is Robert Lundy — Bob for short."

The Sydney home (no.74) has been mentioned before, and next door north lived Mr. and Mrs. Charles Masson and Kathleen. Major Alan and Muriel Gill and their children, Alison, Robert, and Pat resided in no.88, and later the well-known architect George N. Molesworth, his wife, and John, Jill, and David made their home there. This house had at one time been a part of the house on the southwest corner of Colborne Street (no.410 Lakeshore) but had since been considerably altered and enlarged. I remember watching with interest the earlier house being raised slightly above ground-level and placed on a stone foundation, to allow for a full basement underneath. (This operation was carried out on many older houses that lacked basements or cellars, and posed little problem because of the huge squared-timber joists on which they stood. "Away back then" the work was accomplished by means of teams of horses and wagons, and men with picks, shovels, and wheelbarrows. Such undertakings provided jobs for great numbers of the men in town.) After the house was restored, it was occupied by the widow of Dr. W.T. Stuart and her grown children, Jack, Hamilton, and Florence, whose home for many years had been "Holyrood," west of the town. At one period, Colonel and Mrs. Windeyer, Peggy, and Dick had lived in the corner house.

Along Colborne Street the middle house of the three in the block between First and Second streets (no.394) was occupied by the family of Mrs. Fairfield, widow of Mr. James Fairfield, who had formed the Halton Carriage Works in the late 1800s. This firm later became Wm. Whitaker & Sons. Lying west of Mrs. Fairfield's, a large, well-kept lawn gave an unobstructed view from Colborne Street of the pretty stucco house of Mr. and Mrs. L.H. Bedlington, which faced on First Street (no.87). This lawn was part of Mrs. Smith's property, and her home (no.390 Lakeshore) on the southeast corner of First Street is known, historically, as the Captain William Wilson house (1862).

Before passing First Street in the 1900s one would have been well advised to glance down this short street towards the lake. The stately maples lining this particular street may possibly have been slightly superior to others, for it was at the foot of First Street on the west side that Mr. William Francis Romain had built his fine home on the lake in the 1850s (no.40). Being a lover of trees, he had not only planted his own lawn with every available variety, but, as a counciller, had, a few years later, instigated an authorization to be put through the town council to plant all streets and parks in town with maples and other hardy trees. Any trees that died were immediately replaced, and it is certain that much of the beauty of Oakville has been due to Mr. Romain's foresight. It is sad that he lost this home through business failure, but he must have had some satisfaction in watching the town becoming more and more beautiful as his trees matured. (His wife was Esther Ann Chisholm, daughter of William Chisholm, Oakville's founder.) Until his bankruptcy Mr. Romain had been partner with Peter MacDougald when, as grain merchants, they operated the stone "Granary," about which we have heard a great deal in recent years.

In the 1900s Mr. Romain's residence became the home, named "Dungannon," of Mr. and Mrs. W. S. Davis and theirs sons, Douglas ("Dud"), Jim, Bill, Bob, and Ted. Mr. Davis' widespread contributions to the growth of the town cannot possibly be covered here in the space of a few lines. Invaluable to the family, and loved by all who knew him, was John Duncan, who chauffeured Mr. Davis hither and yon throughout his busy life. The second of the two large properties on the west side of First Steet was the handsome house (no.72) occupied

Home of W.S. Davis (W.F. Romain 1855)

Home of Christopher Armstrong (W.E. Hagaman 1850s)

by Mr. and Mrs. Christopher Armstrong and their family, Bob, Marion, Beatrice, Margaret, and Christie. Built in 1855 by Mr. W.E. Hagaman, this large red-brick residence had verandahs on three sides and was surrounded by gardens and fruit and shade trees in grounds that ran through from First to Allan Street. Mr. Armstrong was a partner in the Marlatt and Armstrong Leather Company (the Tannery) on Forsyth Street.

On the east side of First Street at the lake lived Mr. W.G. Jaffray, publisher of the Toronto *Globe*. This house (no.31) had been built in the 1850s by Thomas Jaffray Robertson, who was, among many things, first commodore of the R.C.Y.C. of Toronto. On the southeast corner of Union Street "The Drift Villa-1911" (the name marked over the front door, no.49 First Street) remained unfinished until Mr. W. Ward-Price completed it in the war years. Mr. and Mrs. Ward-Price and their daughters and son, Beryl, Ena, and Ben, proved a great addition to "entertainment" in the town. Some of Mr. Ward-Price's many talents are mentioned in the chapter "Recreation, 1900—1930." As most are aware, Mr. Ward-Price was founder of the famous firm of auctioneers and antique dealers in Toronto. When the Ward-Price family moved elsewhere in 1922, Mr. and Mrs. Harry J. Ahern, "Curly," Doug, and Kitty moved into the Drift Villa. Mr. Ahern, of Thompson Ahern, customs brokers, of Toronto, became a tried-and-true commuter! The house at that time had a particularly wide verandah along the full length of the west side, surrounded by a low wall of lake-stone and supported by large square pillars of the same. This verandah has since been removed. Mrs. Ahern, who was from England, designed her garden along the lines of an English garden, with rose pergola, deep perennial borders, bird-bath, and stone pathways. Members of the Ahern family lived here until the 1960s.

In the 1920s Mr. E. Dean Wilkes built an attractive house for his family in the next block (no. 71). Mr. and Mrs. Wilkes were both keen gardeners and the property around their house was witness to their enthusiasm. Mr. and Mrs. Sheldon Dixon built next on the north (no. 77), and Mr. and Mrs. L.H. Bedington, with Audrey, Lucy, Lyndsie, and Jimmie, occupied what is now no. 87 First Street.

On Colborne Street, at the southwest corner of First Street, was the charming property of Mrs. Herbert Heaven and her son, Arthur. Their house, at the extreme west of the corner lot, was heavily shaded by spruce and cedars, which had grown rather high. Their garden sloped down towards First Street and was secluded, as was the custom for privacy, by a thick cedar hedge. Next door to Mrs. Heaven lived for some years Mr. and Mrs. Walter E. Colwell and Eileen. Theirs was a very attractive, white-stucco house with brown trim, set in a nice garden running to the west. Mrs. Colwell possessed a beautiful soprano voice, and was librarian of the Oakville Public Library for a number of years. It is not possible now to give the exact location of these two fine houses and properties, since the apartment house "Number.-370" Lakeshore Road, has taken their place.

Home of Louis V. Coté, postmaster for 33 years

Mr. Bradbury, contractor, built the two red-brick houses just east of Allan Street in 1911 or thereabouts, and on the southwest corner of this street lived our faithful postmaster of 33 years' standing, Mr. Louis V. Coté, and his wife. Formerly his father's home in the 1800s this house (no.350)[6] was set among lilacs, lily of the valley, forget-me-nots, and other flowers and shrubs. Fruit trees grew at the back, and the garden continued down the slope to Robinson Street. After Mr. Coté moved around the corner to the east side of Allan Street, Miss Florence Delamere and her sister Mrs. Bedlington lived at this corner for a number of years.

Next door a pretty cottage stood on a slightly elevated grass terrace (approximate present location, no.344), the home in the early 1900s of Captain and Mrs. Maurice Fitzgerald, and later of the families of Mr. Gibson, and Mr. McDonald, a prominent carpenter. In

"The What-Not" Antiques (Hilda Gregory)

the 1920s Miss Hilda Gregory operated an attractive antique shop, "The What Not," here. Tea was served regularly and, if weather permitted, on the lawn to the east. Occupying the middle of this block stood the yellow-brick home and office (no.334) of Dr. Charles A. Page, much-loved physician in town. On his death in the 1920s Dr. Page's practice was taken over by Dr. Eric P. Soanes ("Soapie"), who will always live on in the hearts of several generations of his patients and friends. The house on the southeast corner of Reynolds Street (no.326), during this period and beyond, was of red brick with a pretty verandah and gingerbread trim. Among many who occupied this house and corner property were the Fairfield family, the Decker family, Dr. C.M. Oakes, and the family of Dr. Brock Chisholm, who made some alterations to accommodate his patients.

It is an interesting fact that, in 1833, one of Oakville's earliest stores was operated on the southwest corner, by none other than Mr. Charles Reynolds, after whom the street was named. In the very early 1900s McDermott's Barrel Works, or cooperage, stood here. However, in my memory there was an open field between Lakeshore Road and Robinson Street. In the middle of this block lived the Young family: Bob, who in his later years was much sought-after for sharpening lawn-mowers and other cutting-tools; his sister, Winifred, who fitted the ladies of Oakville for "Spirella Corsets"; and a brother,

John. The large house had a wide verandah, deeply shaded by the large maples along Colborne Street, and between the Youngs' wire fence and the house grew a carpet of forget-me-nots, lily of the valley, and clumps of Soloman's seal and ferns.

The house next door[7] was occupied before and during the First World War by the Trotman family. Mr. Trotman, a teamster, was kept busy in his occupation of excavating, raising, and moving houses and other buildings from place to place. His son, Alfie, was a familiar figure in town. Miss Nadine Angstrom then became owner of this house, adding a show-window in front; under the name "The Shuttle," her shop became famous for wools, weaving, and many gifts and artifacts, and it remained in that location for a number of years. Later the building was moved around the corner to the northeast corner of Dundas (Trafalgar) and Robinson streets (no.83 Trafalgar), where Miss Angstrom continued to operate "The Shuttle." The house is notable also for having been the headquarters and workshop of the Oakville Historical Society for some 15 years. It is now owned and well cared for by the Canada Trust Company.

In the early 1920s a very up-to-date theatre, used for both stage productions and moving-pictures, was built at the southeast corner of Colborne and Dundas streets — the present site of the Canada Trust.

Gregory Theatre

The new Gregory Theatre, built after the First World War, filled a great need in Oakville, was the centre of town entertainment for some 30 or 40 years, and was owned and operated by Mr. and Mrs. R. L. Gregory. The four blocks following, from this corner to Navy Street and the creek bank, constituted the business section of town and are described in the chapter "The Main Street."

On the west side of Aberdeen Bridge the construction of ships was always in progress, both during and far beyond the time of the famous builder Captain James Andrew. Entrance to the shipyards was from Forsyth Street, and this street led south to the busy Marlatt and Armstrong Leather Company, where for years so many families earned their living; the area west of the creek contained their homes, built conveniently near their place of employment. West of Forsyth to Kerr Street several houses faced on Colborne Street West (Lakeshore Road), one of which, still standing between Chisholm and Wilson streets, is conspicuous every Spring for the glorious magnolia tree that has bloomed for nearly 100 years in its lovely garden. At the foot of Kerr Street near the lake was Oakville's first reservoir and pumping station,[8] built in the early 1900s. The now grassy site where it stood is still partially visible among the town waterworks buildings in Reservoir Park.

Reservoir and Pumping Station, c.1913

Trees shaded the corner of Brant Street, where the large house and lawn on the east side (now McDonald's) was occupied by the Brown family. Miss Emma Brown was especially well remembered by the hundreds of pupils who passed through her hands at Central School. In later years the home was that of contractor Thomas Shields and his family. Miss Walsh's famous boarding-house stood on the southwest corner, a pretty residence[9] with verandahs and a large garden for the pleasure of the steady stream of summer boarders who returned here year after year. It requires a vivid imagination to superimpose these lovely tree-shaded corner houses upon the present scene.

Home of Percy A. Bath (William Cantley, 1856) (126 Bath Street)

Looking south to the foot of Brant Street was the red-brick house[10] belonging to Mr. Percy Bath (no.126 Bath Street). Mr. and Mrs. Bath were primarily our reason for moving to Oakville from Toronto, where they and my parents had been neighbours. They decided to live 'in the country' and established themselves on their fruit farm, "Belair," along the lakefront between Kerr and Brock streets. We saw a great deal of the Bath family, always spending Sundays with them after church, either in their home or our own. Distance did not seem to deter either family from making the three- or four-mile trip, on roads which were, to say the least, questionable.

To me the Baths' lovely house was like a second home, where the whole family — the three boys, although older, and especially Margaret ("Twitto") — always made me feel as one of them. The centre hall passed a pretty curved staircase on the right and opened into the long, wide living-room, which, with the dining-room adjoining on the right, made up the south side of the house. Many windows looked over lawns, shrubs, and evergreens to the lake beyond, and the roof of the wide verandah along this side was high enough that the rooms were not darkened. Each room upstairs and down had its fireplace, and the large one at the east end of the living-room often blazed with enormous logs. On the Baths' beach I learned to swim; on their lawn I played croquet and other games; and, with the whole family, I enjoyed the happiest of happy times.

Along Lakeshore Road beyond Brock Street stood an attractive one-storey cottage almost hidden by high cedar hedges. This house had been originally a log cabin built by John Terry in the 1830s on his farm "Brock Lands." The cottage, later covered by stucco and occupied by the Brady family, and a large frame-house farther west, belonging in the early 1900s to the McIvor family and then to Mr. Sydney Fearman, were both demolished in the 1960s and replaced by a row of town-houses.

The old part of St. Jude's Cemetery, with its lovely stand of white pine and the wooded lands on the west, had belonged to Mrs. Merrick Thomas before it became the property of the church in 1853. The remainder of the Thomas family's farm and their home (now "The Thomas House" of the Oakville Museum in Lakeside Park) were situated on the north side of Lakeshore Road (now Perdue High School); their wooded property south of the road had been considered unsuitable for farming. A rectory was built on the lakefront here but, after a few years, was found by the clergy to be at an inconvenient distance from the church. Thus a new rectory was erected at Dunn and William streets. The cemetery, however, was put to immediate use. Probably the headstone most familiar to those who pass by now is one near the entrance to the original cemetery, occasionally referred to as "Cleopatra's Needle." The stone marks the grave of Bennett Jull (1844-1916), his wife, Mary E.L. Hagaman (1856-1935), and a four-year-old daughter who died in 1878. Many very old headstones are badly eroded and unreadable, but an early inscription is that of William Triller (1783-1837) and his wife, Sarah (1790-1835).

Dr. William T. Stuart later bought the church property west of the cemetery and resided in the old rectory. He named his new home "Holyrood," enlarged the house considerably, beautified his grounds, and erected a handsome gate at the entrance of the driveway (now Holyrood Avenue) leading from Lakeshore Road through the woods to his home on the lakefront. The Stuart family lived here for several years in the 1900s. In 1912 or thereabouts the outstanding, artistically gifted, and accomplished family of Major Calverley came to live for a few years at the edge of the Holyrood woods (approximate present location, no.304 Lakeshore). In 1924 this property became a part of "Shorewood," the estate of Mr. H. C. Hindmarsh.

Captain Maurice Felan owned the large farm farther along the Lakeshore Road. A retired lake captain, he was an important figure in town — at one time, chief constable; at another, customs collector — and was active in local affairs generally. Next followed the properties of Mr. Orange Ribble and Mr. Powley, and, just east of Appleby School, the summer estate, "Wynwood," of Judge Colin G. Snider of Hamilton. Judge Snider had built at the lakeside a large cottage for his own use, as well as cottages for his son and daughters and their families. The Wynwood gate[11] on Lakeshore Road opened into a large apple orchard, through which the driveway led into a dense wood near the lake, the location of the cottages. I often arrived by Radial Car from Oakville at the car-stop "McCraney's Corners" (Fourth Line) to spend happy hours or days at Wynwood with my good friends the Young family, Mrs. Edith Young being one of Judge Snider's daughters. Appleby College is now owner of most of the Snider property.

Appleby School[12] from 1911 on, stood next west of Wynwood and beyond the Appleby grounds a large McCraney home stood on the south side of the curve at McCraney's Corners. I watched this fine house burn down late in the 1920s. Mr. Burton's farm adjoined the McCraney property on the west, and on the next curve on Lakeshore Road was "Lisonally Farm," the home from the First World War years of Sir Frank and Lady Baillie. Here there was literally not a dull moment. There were horses to ride and a large swimming "tank" as it was called then, with a convenient bungalow for changing. A fine *en-tout-cas* tennis-court was undoubtedly partly responsible for the outstanding tennis played by daughter Marion and her family and friends. This excellent court, when not in use otherwise, was generously made available to the rest of us, regardless of our skill! A very large sun-room along the west side of the house was one of our favourite places for dancing. Lady Baillie's house burned down later on, and was replaced by another on the same site. Next to Lisonally Farm on the west was the home of Mr. W. T. Stirling and his family.

The enjoyment of swimming in the lake at Oakville has already been referred to, and the fact that the beaches in town consisted of shingle (flat stones and pebbles) and flagstone did not seem to detract from it. However, as good luck would have it, those who took the trouble to travel west for a few miles could enjoy swimming, picnics, corn-roasts, and similar pleasures on a long stretch of beautiful sand beach (known to all as "Wilson's Beach") that ran along the shoreline of part of Mr. John Wilson's 210-acre "Gilbrae Farm". Now difficult to identify, covered as it is by residences, the beach would have been situated, roughly speaking, between no.1210 Lakeshore Road and the vicinity of Coronation Park. In the 1930s many Oakville residents built cottages nearby in order to enjoy their summers on the sands. There still stands opposite this popular sandy beach of the past a fringe of trees, the remains of the beautiful "Wilson's Bush," once crammed with wild flowers. Even now in Spring, lovely trilliums may be seen as we speed past the former Wilson's Beach and Bush on the Lakeshore Road West.

Mr. Wilson's first house, at the east end of the present Coronation Park, and his second one, constructed of red brick and situated north of Lakeshore Road, were both located on his large farm, which ran from the lakefront and through the vicinity of the Radial Car tracks (later "the Radial Road"; and Rebecca Street). He owned a prize herd of dairy cattle which supplied fine milk and cream to most of Oakville residents through his son's Gilbrae Dairy. The Wilson family has served the community more than well in affairs of church and school, and has contibuted towards the good of Oakville in general.

Footnotes:

[1] "Hughie" Wilson: grandson of the noted lake captian, William Wilson. (See also pp. 177-8)
[2] Polo field: general area of Ennisclare Drive, east and west.
[3] Now "Gairloch."
[4] This church was in use from 1842 to 1884.
[5] In the 1800s John A. Williams had moved a small office-building to this location, turning it into a residence.
[6] During renovations done in 1980 two distinctly different types of wood sheathing were exposed, revealing that this was first a one-storey house.

[7] Built by Robert Leach, carpenter, in 1837.
[8] Reservoir: see p. 41.
[9] Built in 1854 by Pharis Doty, owner of a sawmill on The Sixteen near the Aberdeen Bridge.
[10] Sometimes referred to as the "Cantley" house, it was built in the 1850s.
[11] Wynwood gate: now Appleby College secondary entrance, east of the main gate.
[12] Appleby School: see pp. 82-85.

"Halfway House" (Barnet Griggs 1828)(No. 1475 Lakeshore E.)

8
Lakeshore Road & Colborne Street (north side)

The vicinity of the Ninth Line (Maplegrove Drive) was our starting point in following the south side of Lakeshore Road and seems also appropriate for the north side. Mention should be made, however, of some of the properties farther to the east, among them the very large estate of Sir Joseph Flavelle (now the location of Charnwood subdivision), which was managed by A. Lofquist, and the homes of the Still family (of Still's Lane), Harry Giddings, who kept a stable of famous racers, Isaac Wilson, and Gordon Gooderham.

The focus for children east of Oakville was the reputable Ninth Line School (later renamed Maple Grove for the fine stand of maple trees surrounding it), and pupils were often to be seen trudging up and down the Ninth Line on their way to and from school.

In the first 20 years or more of the 1900s the land northeast of Lakeshore Road and the Ninth Line was farmed by the brothers James and Ben Waldbrook. Although at the present time surrounded by other houses, the Waldbrook home may still be found as nos. 113-113A Maplegrove. Formerly, the gabled farmhouse stood alone near the corner, among tall trees, and was approached by an avenue from Lakeshore Road. The Waldrooks' farmland along the Ninth Line remained undisturbed until the building boom of the 1950s.

The large farm west of the Ninth Line belonged to Barnet (Barney) Moore, whose home (no.1475) was the original "Halfway House" operated by his grandfather Barnet Griggs from the 1830s as a coach stop. The Moore's home in our time still stood close to the road where, many years before, it had served stage-coaches and their passengers travelling between York (Toronto), Oakville, and Wellington Square (Burlington). A change of horses was made frequently, and relay teams were kept there for that purpose.

Separated from Mr. Moore's property by a small creek, acting as a boundary between the two farms, was the property known as the "Hall Farm," which my father, Vavasor* Robin, owned from 1906. The farm consisted of the large square house (no.1409), a barn, coach-house, and other buildings, standing on 50 acres of fruitland and bush. Our family lived here for a few years after moving from Toronto. A few hundred feet east of our house lived the hired man, Mr. Minnit, and his family from Yorkshire, England.

Mr. James Ryrie, jeweller of Toronto, while creating his estate "Edgemere" between Lakeshore Road and the lake, bought also on the north side of the road Mr. Moore's property as well as my father's. On Mr. Moore's former land, Mr. Ryrie placed the cottage (no.1493) for his estate manager, Mr. Lillie. After the First World War Mr. Ryrie moved Halfway House some distance back from the road, to be occupied by a married son, Harry. Harry and his brother Grant (Jimmy) became well known for their orchards of prize-winning apples which were exported far and wide.

The neighbouring house on our west, one-quarter of a mile away, was a large, brick building (no.1341) set in spacious lawns and covered with Virginia creeper, which trailed down over the wide verandah. This house was owned in the first decade of the 1900s by the Independent Order of Oddfellows, and operated by them as "The Oddfellows Home", a residence for the elderly. I remember seeing its occupants in summer, rocking contentedly on their verandah. The house has been occupied over the years by Colonel W.G. MacKendrick, Mr. J. H. Gundy, Mr. J. R. Pinder, Dr. Crouch, and others.

Before the Lakeshore Road was paved, the bridge over Coates' Creek to the west was a noisy one, containing some loose planks. Until some time after we had moved from the Lakeshore, the Morrison Road was non-existent, still only fields of grazing cattle belonging to the farm of Mr. William Morrison. His red-brick farmhouse, for the most part unchanged today, stands a short distance back from the Lakeshore Road (no.1189). In the approximate area of no.1111 stood a pretty white and green-gabled house, occupied in the early 1900s by Mr. and Mrs. Cruthers and their son and daughter. Judging by the mature trees and hedges that bordered the winding path to the

*A familiar name in the Robin family in the Island of Jersey, Channel Islands. When reference is made to my family, the surname "Robin" is inferred.

verandah at that time, this attractive house had been on the same location for a number of years. The charming "Mrs. C." and my mother were friends and we often visited there. The house was demolished some time in the 1920s.

Standing very close to the road, but half hidden by fence, shrubs, and trees, was the home of Mr. and Mrs. Manbert, Helen, Ray, and Alice (no.1069). The house had been considerably enlarged by Mr. Manbert, who owned several acres north of Lakeshore Road, including "Manbert's Bush" — a fine place for wild-flowers! From here to the Eighth Line (Chartwell Road) were orchards belonging to Mr. W. D. Gregory, who lived on the south side of Lakeshore Road. Halfway between the Eighth Line and Centre Avenue (Balsam Drive) was the property and fine, large home of Mr. W.H. Speers (no.509), a director of the Oakville Navigation Company, owners of the ill-fated steamship *White Star*.[1] Later this residence became the home of Mr. J.M. Wallace, sometime owner of the Oakville Basket Factory. Mr. Wallace was instrumental in the development of the lighted baseball diamond at Wallace Park.[2] At some time between 1910 and 1920 Mr. Speers built a house (no.489) on his property to the west of his residence.

In the early 1900s Mr. Carrique lived for several years at the northeast corner of Centre Avenue in a house built earlier by Mr. George Andrew and named "Clearview" (no.109 Balsam Drive). This property followed the pattern of so many others in town, that of a charming, well-proportioned house set on beautifully kept lawns, with flower-gardens, hedges, and many trees. The present line of very tall trees south of this house was, in Mr. Carrique's time, a young, well-trimmed hedge. Mr. Carrique, dressed in black coat and fedora, both serving to set off his white beard, could be seen almost daily in his light "democrat," drawn by his small horse, jogging to and from the downtown.

On the northwest corner of Centre Avenue stood the imposing white frame-house (no.457 Lakeshore) built by Mr. William Wass in the 1870s in the southwest section of his property. His choice of the name "Balsam Lawn" for his home was appropriate, for it was surrounded by a lovely stand of pine, spruce, and balsam. The house was barely visible through these beautiful trees, and the garden they enlosed was a picture of decorative shrubs and trimmed evergreens. For the first quarter of the 1900s Miss Rebecca Wass occupied Balsam Lawn alone.

"Balsam Lawn" (Wass family home)

Centre Avenue was the name chosen in the 1800s by Mr. William Wass since that road ran through the centre of his farm. Although the long road reached from the Lakeshore Road to what is now MacDonald Road, and although over the years Mr. Wass gradually disposed of his property, Centre Avenue had, until the First World War years, just seven land-owners, the residences of whom could be reached only by driveways leading from Centre Avenue. Those properties on the west side of the road ran through to the future location of Gloucester Avenue, which was not open to traffic until 1913—15.

At the south end of Centre Avenue, on the east side, the first farm north of the corner house was that of Mr. George Tailby, who lived there with his wife, Charlie, and Laura in the residence that is now no.159 Balsam. The first house on the west side (no.148), within part of what remained of the Wass estate, was occupied by the family of Mr. Brooman, who maintained the property for Miss Rebecca Wass for several years. Mr. Harry Husband's home (no.184) stood to the north, followed by Mr. George Oliphant's fine farm of good, rich loam, which extended from a short distance south of Palmer Avenue up to some 200 feet north of Sheddon Avenue. Moorcroft Drive was formed in the 1950s slighly to the north of the driveway which had led to Mr. Oliphant's farmhouse (no.237 Gloucester).

My father's fruit farm occupied the area extending from Mr. Oliphant's property line north of Sheddon up to (and including) the then non-existent MacDonald Road. There was no right of way at the north end of my father's property, and a path through it was used as a short-cut by those on foot. A road joined Centre Avenue and the Eighth Line, and vehicles used these north-south roads to reach the Lakeshore. The driveway leading to our house (no.317 Gloucester) opened off Centre Avenue at the approximate location of no.316 Balsam Drive. We were fortunate in the fact that, before we moved there, Galt Avenue had been laid out as part of the "Brantwood Survey," and although the roadway was poor, we had a sidewalk leading directly to our house.

On the east side of Centre Avenue stood a house (no.275 Balsam) that is little changed today. This was the home for many years of Mr. and Mrs. George Crossley, Kathleen, Vera, Mary, Dorothy, Nora, and Dick. Dorothy (later Denison) is familiar to many as the popular curator of the Oakville Museum in the 1950s and 1960s. Nora will be remembered for her reputation as a top player in tennis, badminton, and golf and as an expert in art and handcrafts. Dick, who was a member of the Forestry Department, is to be gratefully remembered by present residents of Balsam Drive for planting the many trees which now beautify the area of the former Crossley property. After the war two houses were built nearby and occupied by members of the family.

The tall spruce trees now lining Balsam Drive farther north were planted in 1915-16 as a small hedge beside the summer cottage built at that time by Mr. Alex Mills of Toronto. This "cottage" has now become no.333 Balsam Drive! During these same years the Reverend W.B. Caswell built a small summer residence at the southeast corner of MacDonald Road. Finally, facing south to overlook the full length of Centre Avenue, stood the large, brick home of Mr. and Mrs. Davey

Chapman, Ruby, and Bob. Later, Perkins and Son Greenhouses operated here. The approximate site of the house, demolished in the 1970s, is no.465 MacDonald.

At Gloucester Avenue a brief outline of the Brantwood Survey might be appropriate. Up to the year 1902 Mr. C.W. Anderson lived in a rather pretentious home, demolished in the 1960s, on the northeast corner of Allan Street. He ran a successful farm of some 200 acres east of Allan and north of Colborne Street, and, with his son, operated a private bank in his own prominent brick building on Colborne near Navy (nos.126—34). However, Anderson's Bank failed tragically in 1902, and the family lost, not only their fine building on "the Main Street," but their handsome home and large area of farmland on the eastern fringe of the town. This bank failure spelled tragedy for a great number of Oakville residents, many of whom lost their savings in the disaster. The Bank of Hamilton (later the Canadian Bank of Commerce) was the principal creditor in the bankruptcy and, to help recover its losses, the board of directors planned a large "subdivision," Brantwood Survey, on Mr. Anderson's farmland. In charge of opening up this project — planning the streets, sewers, and sidewalks and selling the lots — was the Cumberland Land Company, and their chief agent was Mr. W. S. Davis, who was also local manager of the Bank of Hamilton.

Brantwood Survey was bounded by what became Gloucester Avenue and by Colborne, Allan, and Spruce streets. By 1909 roads had been laid out and graded, and sparkling new cement sidewalks ran north, south, east, and west. Within a few years sewers and waterworks were added. On Colborne Street, around 1916, the entrances to Brantwood were indicated by large, square, grey-stone pillars, placed one at either side of Gloucester, Watson, and Douglas avenues. These pillars lent quite an air of elegance to Colborne Street East, and the roadside looked bare when it was decided to tear them down in the 1940s or 1950s. Although all the services were in readiness, houses in Brantwood Survey were at first rather conspicuous by their absence. In 1911—12, however, by dint of much advertising and the untiring and professional efforts of Mr. W. S. Davis, this very large survey began to fill up. Even in this one venture alone, Mr. Davis' success in real estate cannot be over-emphasized.

There was at first no sign that there was ever to be a Gloucester Avenue, even though the other Brantwood streets had been graded and provided with sidewalks, and it was not until 1912—13 that the road allowance was cut through the dense bush up to the northern

Gloucester Avenue c.1915, looking south

boundary, Spruce Street. The decision to open up Gloucester at this time was made because the long-hoped-for paving of the Toronto-Hamilton Highway was shortly to be extended to Oakville from Toronto. This may seem, at first glance, a rather remote reason for developing Gloucester Avenue, but the fact was that since all the heavy materials needed for construction of the highway would be coming by rail, some means had to be found for their transportation from the railway tracks down to the Lakeshore Road. Since all the north-south streets in town were built up by this time, albeit some only sparsely, this task could be accomplished with the least inconvenience to residents by use of the Gloucester Avenue right of way, which had no houses on it. The west side was still bush, consisting of mature trees and underbrush, while the four properties on the east fronted on Centre Avenue.

Accordingly, a narrow-gauge track was laid the length of the newly cleared Gloucester Avenue from the Grand Trunk (C.N.) railway tracks down to Colborne Street, and on it a small steam "donkey-engine," with a long string of dump-trucks in tow ran a frequent shuttle service, carrying all supplies throughout the local construction of the highway. The Toronto-Hamilton Highway was completed through Oakville in 1915. It may be that not very many of the townspeople realized that all this was taking place in their usually peaceful "Anderson's Bush," as it was called. However, I lived then on my father's nine-acre fruit farm on Centre Avenue (now no.317 Gloucester) and witnessed all these exciting happenings with my very own eyes!

On Colborne Street the block between Gloucester and Watson avenues consisted of two small hills, each sloping towards the middle of the block, where a small stream ran. From there the stream passed under Colborne Street and then on towards the lake through the "Raymar" estate. The more important, or higher, of these hills was at the northeast corner at Watson Avenue and was named "Anderson's Hill." From the first snowfall to the last, it was the haunt of every child in town as a winter playground. The summit of the hill at the corner was somewhat fan-shaped, giving an almost unlimited area for "take-off" down a pretty good slope on your choice of sleigh, bob-sleigh, or toboggan, everyone ending up in the vicinity of Gloucester Avenue. This may be a difficult scene to visualize now, since at some point in "progress" the removal of several feet of earth from the top of the hill ended, for all time, this "winter wonderland."

Mr. Isaac Warcup, former owner of the grist mill, lived in retirement in the brick house at the northwest corner of Watson Avenue (no.407). He had contributed to the long success of the mill by constructing above it a large dam, about 170 feet in length, to offset the decrease in the flow of water in The Sixteen caused by deforestation. Mr. Warcup died in 1924 at the age of 87; until the end, he was at work on his life-long hobby, the search for the solution to the theory of "perpetual motion." Only three houses occupied the block between Watson and Douglas Avenue until the late 1920s: Mr. Warcup's was one; Mrs. McGee (later Mrs. Detmold) and her three attractive daughters lived in the centre house (no.401); and the northeast corner of Douglas (no.389) was the home for some years of Dr. and Mrs. Dingle and their son, the famous artist Adrian Dingle.

The lovely Finch-Noyes property, comprising the block from Colborne to Randall Street and from Allan Street to Douglas Avenue, boasted huge trees surrounding a large, white frame-house of unusual architecture. Lovely lawns and smaller trees in the vicinity of the house were contained by a white picket fence. White gates at the corner of Colborne and Allan streets opened onto a shaded driveway leading to the house, and an entrance at the east end of Church Street led to the stables and the back of the house. The land at the Douglas-Colborne corner was very low-lying and, being fed by springs, was marshy and overgrown with bulrushes and swamp-grass. The house had been the

Finch-Noyes home
(demolished 1960s, northeast corner Allan & Lakeshore E.)

residence of C.W. Anderson until the failure of his private bank in 1902. Mr. J. T. Madden and his family lived here for a few years until E. Finch-Noyes from Hamilton bought the property in 1911. The lovely old house was demolished in the 1960s and a large apartment complex now covers this block.

The next two residential blocks — between Allan and Dundas (Trafalgar Road) — were closely lined with the mixture of hard and soft maples which Mr. W. F. Romain had had planted throughout the town in the 1870s. Since Colborne Street was not widened until a good many years later, wide grass boulevards on either side of the cement sidewalks contributed to making it one of many pleasant residential streets in Oakville. It may be difficult now to picture this area as anything but solid masonry.

Pete and Annie Shaughnessy, and later their brother, Father Shaughnessy, lived on the west corner of Allan Street in a pretty, two-storey, brick house, trimmed in white; it had the customary verandah

Lakeshore Road looking east from Reynolds Street

and Virginia creeper, and hedges for privacy. In the middle of this block was a large, red-brick, Victorian house. White-trimmed and decorated liberally with gingerbread trim, it was set in a particularly picturesque lawn conspicuous for its many flowering almond, cherry, and crab-apple trees as well as for its copper beeches. A decorative coach-house stood in the northeast corner of the property. This was the home of Mr. and Mrs. Wyatt S. Wood and their daughters, Monica and Frances.

In 1830 a large house stood at the northeast corner of Reynolds and Colborne streets. It had been constructed by William Uptegrave, builder and successful proprietor of the Royal Exchange Hotel on the Main Street. In 1856 Joseph Milbourne, owner of the tannery Joseph Milbourne and Company, lived here; his firm was the forerunner of the Marlatt and Armstrong Leather Company. In the latter part of the 1800s this corner house was divided into two stucco dwellings, which stood side by side on the same location for a great many years. The one on the corner of Reynolds Street still remains (no.321 Lakeshore). In 1965, however, the easterly of the two, which had contained the original staircase from the 1830 house, was demolished in favour of stores. In it had lived, in my memory, Jesse F. Humphrey, shoe-dealer, and in 1922 I.N. Tompkins, manager of the "new" Royal Bank of Canada; from some time later in the 1920s the family of Dennis J.

321 Lakeshore Road
(William Uptegrave 1829)(V. Robin 1920-1940s)

(Jim) Sullivan, prominent Oakville electrician, grew up here. In 1920 my father had the corner house raised to accommodate a full basement and furnace; he also added a fireplace and bay-window, rearranged some of the interior upstairs and downstairs, and placed a verandah along the east side. There we lived comfortably from 1920 to 1945. I am happy to see that the basic house is preserved, after its life of 150 years, and can still be recognized above the surrounding one-storey shops on the corner.

The same can be said for the Alec Chisholm house on the opposite corner of Reynolds Street. This was such a well-proportioned, satisfying style of family home that, in spite of camouflaging, the original house can still be recognized, if with some difficulty, by those who knew it well. Mr. Alec Chisholm was a successful lawyer of long standing in Oakville, and all his children — Dorothy, Ruth, Donald, Kenneth, Charles, and Alec — were born and brought up in this house. Their garden reached to Church Street from the back of the house and was surrounded by a high board-fence. The Chisholms' property west along Colborne Street, together with part of Mr. Alexander ("Sandy") MacDonald's garden next door, has been covered by the Odeon Theatre (now "The Playhouse"). The core of Mr. MacDonald's home (no.305) is still intact and surrounded by small stores. For years Sandy MacDonald was one of Oakville's busiest blacksmiths; his shop was in the middle of the next block.

Dr. R. O. Fisher, our first family doctor, and his pretty wife, Blossom, lived in the next house (approximate present location, no.299). When we still lived down the Lakeshore, I remember the nice Dr. Fisher driving at night by horse and cutter to look after some now long-forgotten childhood ailment of mine. When Dr. Fisher moved his practice to Toronto, around 1915, Dr. John H. Stead succeeded him in the same home and office, remaining there until the late 1950s. Dr. Stead was Medical Office of Health for a number of years and was a very busy and popular doctor. (A fond remembrance here of Dr. Stead's wife, Olive, and his three step-children, Gerald, Eric, and Betty O'Reilly.) Beside Dr. Stead's was a house that belonged to the Conder family; set back from the street, it became after the First World War years Bill Hill's Grocery Store. Mr. and Mrs. Bill Hill were real friends to every one of their customers — and they were legion!

Early in the 1900s, at the northeast corner of Dundas Street, a large brick house arose on the ashes of the short-lived Commins' Music Hall. This entertainment hall of almost unbelievable architecture survived only four years of what were, according to historical accounts, never-to-be-forgotten performances before it burned to the ground in 1898. The house replacing it (now the site of the Toronto-Dominion Bank) was shaded by a tree on the corner that stood, inconveniently, on the sidewalk-line; but a tree was treasured then, so

Trafalgar Road and Lakeshore E. c.1912 (looking east)

the sidewalk was divided at that point and the tree continued to flourish. Other trees grew beside the house along Dundas Street, and two symmetrical blue spruce stood on either side of the front entrance. This seemed always to be the home and office of a long succession of dentists, perhaps the best remembered being doctors C.E. Williams, L.A. Jaques, and W.P. Jebb.

The four blocks west of Dundas Street constituted the Main Street, or business section of the town, and are dealt with in the following chapter. Before we pick up Colborne Street at the Aberdeen Bridge across The Sixteen mention should be made of the town garbage dump,[3] which was situated immediately north of the Lakeshore Road bridge and at the bottom of the east river-bank. This was an on-going embarrassment to the town but, since no other site could be found, teams of horses continued to pull the full and empty garbage wagons up and down a separate roadway at the south end of the Public School playground. The school children, on the whole, ignored this rather unsavoury depository in such close proximity and, in fact, welcomed a good snowfall, when they scrambled down the hill to find suitable pieces of tin or heavy cardboard on which to slide down this good slope on the east river-bank. A south wind, which fortunately blew very seldom, could waft into the school windows a rather sour "garbage smell," and also the much stronger smell blowing from the Marlatt and Armstrong Leather Company, as it processed and tanned the leather. This was known to all as "the Tannery smell," and although I have tried, I have never found anyone who could describe it.

From the Aberdeen Bridge one noticed a very slight slope up what was, in reality, the west bank of the river. Along this slope, on the north side between Forsyth and Chisholm streets ran the property of Mr. and Mrs. Robert King and son, Gordon. The Kings' gabled house at the top of the incline was surrounded by trees, shrubs, and a pretty garden, and their property thus made a pleasant scene leading away from The Sixteen. A. LeBarre's Grocery Store at the northwest corner of Chisholm Street was a landmark for many years; it was later the grocery store of Mr. J.M. Campbell, at one time Mayor of Oakville.

After several "ups and down," typical of the establishment of most churches, the African Methodist Episcopal Church was built in 1892 between Chisholm and Wilson streets; it was supported by faithful members in both Bronte and Oakville. I knew personally one of the ministers of this church, the Reverend Joshua Wickard Edgehill, a fine, well-educated gentleman from Jamaica. His three daughters, who attended Central School when I did, were fine Jamaican girls: excellent students full of fun and a joy to be with — especially my favourite, Julia!

Past Wilson Street, a large house standing close to the sidewalk was occupied by the family of Mr. and Mrs. H. Farr, and at the corner of Kerr Street lived the Ribble family. Beyond this, my memory is not very clear, although at the time I knew enough to turn up Brant Street to go to the Oakville Fair Grounds! Mr. William McPherson, hardware expert with James N. McGregor (no.234 Lakeshore), lived with his family close to Brock Street.

There can be only a few in Oakville who do not know the history of the Merrick Thomas house, and those who wish to know more may easily obtain information at the Oakville Museum, of which "The Thomas House" is a part. In our period, 1900—30, this home was the residence of Mr. and Mrs. A Skoog and their family. It was an attractive house, very many sizes larger than the Thomas House in Lakeside Park, since the latter is only the Thomas family's first, or pioneer, home. The Skoogs' property consisted of rolling ground, well covered by evergreens and other trees; the Perdue High School and grounds cover this farm property now.

Many acres in the vicinity of Morden Road were owned by members of the Morden family. Although a few names of the family come to mind — William H., E.A., Hardy, George, and Campbell — I realise that there were many others and apologise for not being able to name them in their proper order. The two-storey brick house with mansard roof that is now no.417 Lakeshore Road had been reconstructed to its attractive proportions by Captain Hugh F. Pullen, R.N., Hazel Mathews tells us, and "after the turn of the century, passed into the hands of Captain G.H. Morden." Another fine Morden home (no.491) stood at the northeast corner of the present Suffolk Drive. This outstanding family was noted for its important role in many local affairs of town and township.

The McCraney homestead (no.549) and property north of Lakeshore Road had been part of the family's large land-holdings from the first years of settlement in that area. Many acres had bordered on the Fourth Line: hence the old name McCraney's Corners for the junction of Lakeshore Road and the Fourth Line. One year after Appleby School opened in 1911, it leased this house and property, which lay across from the school, to accommodate an unexpectedly large number of boys enrolling for the second year.

One of the last homes in our description of the Lakeshore Road from the Ninth to the Fourth Line of the old Township of Trafalgar is the present no.573 Lakeshore, which was, before its present restoration, a particularly fine example of the architecture of the 1900—30 period. At the time that Appleby School was opening across the road, two maiden ladies from Toronto, the Windeat sisters, commissioned the young architect George N. Molesworth to design their three-storey home (one of the many designed by him in Oakville), and it was as delightful inside as it was out. The spot may have been chosen for the number of fine trees growing there, and the name given the house, "The Acacias," was the result of the predominance of several of that species. McCraney's Creek, running through the McCraney property and on through the Appleby grounds to the lake, passed by the bottom of their garden. Hidden from the highway by clever landscaping with hedges and shrubs, this attractive house nestled among the trees until it passed from the hands of Mr. H. L. Wethey's family in the 1970s; it had been their charming home for more than 30 years.

A very short distance north of the Lakeshore Road the Fourth Line crossed the Radial Car tracks, and on the right began the beautiful property of Mr. Aubrey Heward. McCraney's Creek trickled through the landscaped lawns beside lush beds of flowers, and rose-gardens producing the prize-winning blooms that brought Mr. Heward fame at Rose Shows everywhere. These gardens followed the Fourth Line up to the driveway, which led to the terraces on which his large house stood, until recent years, overlooking the grounds. Mr. Heward grew also prize-winning apples and other fruit.

Farther north on the Fourth Line, accommodating the pupils west of Oakville, the original Pine Grove School[4] stood in a lovely grove of pine trees — the counterpart of Maple Grove School, with its surrounding maple trees, on the Ninth Line east of Oakville!

Footnotes:

[1] White Star pp. 60-61.
[2] Wallace Park: formerly called Victoria Park, pp. 71-72.
[3] Many years later the area was covered in and became a popular softball park, named Busby Park in honour of William Busby, who had been one of many promoters untiring in their efforts to have the "dump" moved elsewhere.
[4] Pine Grove School: now barely visible as no.607 Stephen Crescent.

"Medical Hall"—Dr. John Urquhart

9
"The Main Street"

From the corner of Colborne and Dundas streets (Lakeshore and Trafalgar roads) through to Navy Street was the business section of the town, and was usually referred to as "the Main Street." The south side remained residential and was shaded with beautiful maple trees as far as Knox Presbyterian Church, but horse-chestnuts and other shade-trees grew also at intervals in front of the shops on the north side. Until the time that motor cars really began to outnumber horse-drawn vehicles, roughly around 1911—12, many of the stores still had their hitching-posts at the sidewalk's edge. Until it was paved in 1915 the surface of the street left something to be desired. In dry weather horse-drawn watering-carts toiled slowly up and down the Main Street, as well as the "back streets," wetting down the dust. After a rain mudguards were a definite necessity on all vehicles, whether horse-drawn or motorized, and also on the numerous bicycles. The first known speed limit for cars was 10 m.p.h. in towns, 15 m.p.h. on the open road.

SOUTH SIDE

Dr. J.S.W. Williams' large, red-brick house and office stood at the southwest corner of Dundas Street, with its well-used verandah and a white picket fence enclosing a garden consisting mostly of shrubs. Dr. Williams' "surgery," which had its own entrance, faced Dundas Street South. An Esso station now stands on this corner property. Dr. Williams' wife and my mother were good friends and we often had tea there. I don't remember meeting Dr. Williams at home;

he would have been too busy making house-calls, many of which were several miles out in the country, and acting as well as Medical Officer of Health and Coroner. I do, however, recall vividly seeing the doctor being trotted about town by horse and buggy — very distinguished by his snow-white beard.

What is now no. 270 was once the home of Mr. Frank Chisholm's family and later the real-estate office of Messrs. T.R. Jarvis and J.A. Cowie. Next door was the residence[1] of Mr. Charles Decker's family (no.266, now Ramsay Drugs). Knox Presbyterian Church, with its handsome architecture and prominent steeple, dominated the tree-shaded corner of Dunn Street, as it had since 1888. The tall, brick, three-storey building across Dunn Street (no.240) was a "high-class" furniture store, owned and operated for at least the first 30 years of this century by Mr. Peter Kelley and his family. They lived in the upper apartments, which could be reached from within the store as well as by a separate outside entrance off the sidewalk. A good-sized lawn separated the Kelley building from the hardware store of James N. McGregor next door.

James N. McGregor's Hardware Store (no.234) was one of the busy early hardware stores in Oakville. It seemed to me that my father and I spent an interminable time here on each visit to town, all the while nearly asphyxiated by the strong smell of coal-oil. However, Mr. and Mrs. McGregor were very pleasant and always seemed to find time to be nice to a small child like me, trailing along after her father. Small hardware of every description was kept in labelled drawers and bins, to be counted out or weighed for the customer. Great rolls of this and that were unwound, measured, and cut with enormous shears, and endless panes of glass were cut before your very eyes. Opinions had, of course, to be exchanged at great length on the merits and quality of each product. And always there was the pervading smell of coal-oil!

Householders who still used coal-oil lamps brought their own galvanized gallon-cans frequently for a refill. Many by this time were using four-burner, coal-oil cook-stoves, with separate oven, as an auxiliary to their coal-burning stoves, and for these a five-gallon can would be needed, delivered by McGregor's horse and wagon. (Town merchants all maintained their own delivery service.) Gradually both methods of cooking were replaced by electricity and, in the 1920s, by gas, which was piped to Oakville from Hamilton. Mr. McGregor also carried on tinsmithing, plumbing, and other activities, kept a good stock of stoves, furnaces, and builders' supplies, and employed a sizeable number of workers the year round.

For a few years during the 1920s Mr. W.R. Grammell operated a men's clothing and tailor shop to the west of Mr. McGregor's (no.232); he was also an agent for Hobberlin's men's wear. Thomas Nisbet,[2] a strikingly tall, handsome gentleman with a very black beard, had an optician's shop next door (no.226). The proprietor as well of "Oakville's leading 'Musical Emporium'," where it was possible to obtain "any musical instrument from a Jew's Harp to a Player Piano," Mr. Nisbet was also local representative of the Singer Sewing Machine Company and looked after all their repairs. A very busy man.

To the west of Mr. Nisbet, J. Wesley Kelley operated a bicycle and general repair shop (no.224); the home of Mr. Kelley and his fine family lay at the rear of the same premises. Across a wide driveway stood a large one-storey building of rough grey stone (approximate present location, nos.216-18) which extended some distance back from the sidewalk and was known familiarly as "McGregor's Stove Store." This large warehouse was an adjunct of McGregor's Hardware Store and contained his larger items of merchandise, such as stoves and furnaces. It served also as his workshop for tinsmithing, plumbing, heating, and repairs.

"Royal Exchange Hotel"
(built 1829) (approximately 217 Lakeshore E.)

On the last half of this block stood the remains of the ancient Royal Exchange Hotel,[3] once a large and bustling coach exchange in Oakville, but in the 1900s in rather poor repair. The only remaining tenant that I was aware of was Mr. Sam Wo, who was in competition with Mr. Charlie Chung for the townspeople's hand-laundry business. We favoured Sam Wo who was believed to lose, on the whole, fewer articles of clothing than his competitor. Only articles needing special starching, such as men's collars and shirts and a few women's stiffened collars and shirtwaists, were taken to the hand-laundry. Everything else was done once a week on a grand scale at home by the current "washer-woman" — or possibly sent out to Mrs. Rose Lawrence, Mrs. Fixter, or others, to be done expertly in their own homes. The arrival in 1911 of the Appleby boys with their Eton collars, I'm sure, improved business for the Chinese hand-laundry! A small torn piece of paper, bearing some Chinese characters, would redeem your laundry in a week's time, provided you had not lost it. The large stone building built as Oakville's Fourth Post Office (no.216) stands today roughly where the eastern end of the Royal Exchange Hotel was located.

The store at the southwest corner of George Street (no. 202) was operated by Mr. Art Thomas, who was somewhat of a mechanical and electrical genius. After Mr. Thomas moved to other quarters, George Ramsay's Cigar Store remained in business on the corner for 20 or more years. Unfortunately, the building was destroyed by fire in January 1981. Just past the corner of George Street (and also destroyed in this fire) was the Oakville Public Library (no.198), sternly presided over by Mrs. Irvine, the librarian. A good-sized reading-room contained two large tables spread with the latest periodicals — the *Illustrated London News*, the *Sketch*, the *Tatler*, *Punch*, the *Delineator*, and, last but not least, the *Ladies' Home Journal*. There were also reference books here, and a large dictionary on a stand. The reading-room was a popular stopping-place, but some complained that it was too convenient a spot to sit and watch the world go by on the Main Street outside the window, or to meet a friend — although anything above a whisper was condemned, and even a whisper frowned upon!

Past Mrs. Irvine's desk at the back was the lending library, a large shelf-filled room containing hundreds of adults' and children's books, both fact and fiction. In addition to the classics, authors or authoresses for adults might include Rider Haggard, Baroness Orczy, Booth Tarkington, Ethel M. Dell, Michael Arlen, and P.G. Wodehouse, to name a few. Children's "series" were in vogue: one harrowing volume after another of "Elsie Dinsmore"; the "Marjorie" books; the "Katy" books; "Little Women"; "the Little Colonel"; "Campfire Girls"; "Hardy Boys"; adventure stories for boys by G. A. Henty; "Chums"; and "Boys Own Paper." According to age and taste there were books by Gene Stratton Porter, L.T. Meade, Edgar Rice Burroughs, Rosa N. Carey, Frances Hodgson Burnett, and Louisa M. Alcott. The fine for an overdue book? One cent per day — and no excuse accepted!

Mrs. Moulton's Candy and Grocery Store (in that order of importance, if you were a child) was next to the library (no.196), and the street door rang a bell as you entered. Soon Mrs. or Miss Moulton would appear from their living -quarters at the rear to attend to your wants. I believe that most of the staples in the grocery line were available here, and my mother contended that Mrs. Moulton's butter was second to none in the town; however, the ceremony of "tasting before buying" would not be omitted under any circumstances, by either grocer or customer. (With ice refrigeration in use, the butter might have been tainted.)

As may be seen today, Mrs. Moulton's was a small store, and precautions had been taken inside to protect from the young customer's grasp the tempting display of "one-cent-candy," to be seen in the shop-window from the sidewalk. An ingenious barricade of large Christie Biscuit tins accomplished this: a child had to stand on one row of these tins and, peering over a second row, point with a finger to his choice or choices. These were then placed in a paper bag (sometimes into a "cornucopia" of paper) by either Mrs. or Miss Moulton. They showed infinite patience with the steady stream of town children, who, during a five-cent purchase of "cent candy," would, quite probably, have changed their minds ten times.Grab-bags and Cracker Jack were popular for the element of surprise. Liquorice in the form of whips and plugs of tobacco, chocolate-coated marshmallow brooms and mice, large "marbles" made in layers which changed colour as you sucked them, tiny "Midgets" in a box, and Mrs. Moulton's home-made fudge and taffy made decisions difficult.

Mrs. Moulton's husband, George, had been a ship's captain on the Great Lakes for many years. Her brother, E.H. Gulledge, operated a leather shop next door, the same location in which their father, Henry Gulledge, saddler and harness-maker, had started in business in 1835. E.H. Gulledge had moved here after fire destroyed his original premises on the southeast corner of Thomas Street and the Lakeshore Road. He was an expert in harness and leather repairs of all kinds. An Oakville newspaper noted in 1906:

> "E.H. Gulledge is installing a wax thread harness stitching-machine in his harness store. This will be run by a new gasoline engine. Other machinery will also be introduced. Mr. Gulledge has a most complete shop."

The workshop referred to adjoined his shoe store and was entered by stepping down a few steps into it from the main store, or from the sidewalk outside. It was indeed a busy place in the days when so many horses needed almost continuous repairs to their harnesses. With my luck, my father and I often ended up in the lower regions of the harness repair shop, where all was serious business. I would have preferred to have been next door having a look at things in the shoe store. (The two stores occupied the present nos.190—94.)

In a small building to the west (no.188) Ollie Johnson both lived and operated a dry-cleaning and pressing shop for more years than I can guess at. Ollie made a name for himself in Oakville history as a famous runner and all-round athlete — particularly in baseball — and is remembered above all for his very wide circle of friends. William Joyce's General Store (no.184) was a busy place, selling groceries, flour and feed, boots, shoes, and clothing. His horse and delivery wagon were to be seen at all hours of the day delivering his merchandise.

No.182 Lakeshore has a great distinction, although most passers-by today do not know of it. This building was Medical Hall, where Dr. John Urquhart was born, and where he remained for most of his 89 years. His father had opened a drug business here in the 1830s. The drug store was large and spotlessly clean, and more than a drug store, since its owner was a doctor as well as a chemist. Three walls were lined with shelves holding rows of labelled jars and bottles, of both glass and ceramic. Many of these have been preserved and are now highly treasured. Small bottles containing curative drugs, tinctures, and so on were ranged near the counter at the left, where Dr. Urquhart mixed and filled prescriptions; he also manufactured all his own pills. He measured out mysterious powders and liquids on his brass scale and the ingredients would then be mixed (I remember a mortar and pestle) and either wrapped in small white papers, with ends neatly turned under, or bottled. A few stools were provided for customers who waited.

Dr. Urquhart served long, faithfully, and efficiently and was loved by a great many people in Oakville. The following letter, written in his hand, was sent to Hazel Mathews by his daughter, Mrs. Evelyn (Urquhart) McCleary, whose home is in Oakville. The letter was written in 1929 when he was 85, and is a highly valued outline of his life.

Oakville, April 20th, 1929

The Financial Times
651 Craig Street West
Montreal

Sirs:

". . . My father was Druggist. Came to Canada in 1830; landed at New York, U.S.A.; too much of a loyalist to stay in New York and when he was offered a good position he eventually came to Toronto when it was Muddy York. Was compelled to go out to West Guillambury to teach school to keep him from starvation. Could get no occupation in Toronto. When the Cholera struck Toronto in 1832, he went up before the Licensing Board and qualified to practise Medicine and almost wore himself out attending patients. He eventually started a Drug Store in Toronto on King Street in partnership with a Doctor by name of Reath if my memory serves me right — but they failed in business and the Sheriff sold them out for rent, which completely broke him financially.

"He came to Oakville. When Ship Fever attacked emigrants from Ireland and Scotland the Government established a hospital in Oakville on the west side of the river of which he had charge. What was described as Ship Fever was Typhus Fever contracted by being too closely confined in the hold of the ship on account of storms, which sometimes last for 3 and 4 days, when all passengers were kept below in the ship's hold. Having no convenience, the atmosphere became poisonous. That was the cause of the Ship Fever or Typhus.

"He opened an office on Colborne Street, Oakville, between the years of 1832 and 1836. I myself studied the drug business under his tutelage; manufactured all his pills, tinctures and powders and carried on his Drug Business for 20 years. In the meantime I conceived the idea of going in for Medicine and attended Dr. Rolph Medical College which was in affiliation with Victoria College, Toronto, in the year 1864 to 1867.

"My Father died on the 22nd day of June 1867, and I carried on the Drug Business for 12 or 13 years. Went back to Trinity Med. Coll. and passed my final Examination in 1882. Fellow of Trinity Med. School, Trinity Coll. M.D., M.M., D.G.M., in 1883. Went to Edinboro in 1882, passed the L.R.C.P. and L.M. Came back to Canada and got my certificate M.C., P.G.O. Canada, also Licence from Edinboro 1882.

"Been in Oakville all my life; born in the year 1844, January 31; am now in my 86 year; hale and hearty, only getting a little stiff in my muscles when I sit in one position too long.

"I might say my Father was a self-educated man: held the rush-light

> when his Mother spinned at night, while he studied his books qualifying himself to go out in the Highlands of Scotland to teach school. He worked on the Duke of Sutherland's Estate when a young boy."

Mrs. McCleary gives us this account of her father's part in the serious smallpox epidemic of 1907:

> "Father was the one who recognized the first case as being smallpox, and soon it had spread all over town. He had a 'camp' set up on the west side of the river, on the lakefront near Holyrood, and everyone who developed the disease had to be taken there until they were better. The patients were picked up one by one and driven through town by horse and wagon (resembling a 'lumber-wagon') to the camp, where they were looked after. When people saw one of these wagons, they knew it was a case of smallpox and took care not to go near. I do not know how many contracted the disease, nor how long the camp was necessary, because Father decided to take the precaution of sending me away, and I was out of Oakville when the epidemic was at its worst."

Several years after Dr. Urquhart's retirement, two enterprising brothers of Italian origin, Mat and Tony Palumbo from Toronto, operated a successful fruit- and vegetable-stand from the same location. Mat Palumbo carried on this business for a number of years here, and he and Mrs. Palumbo lived in their fine apartment on the second floor.

High up on the outside east wall of the building at present occupied by P & L Office Supply the outline of a peaked roof may still be seen; the very old store that supported it was demolished in the 1960s, (approximate present location, no.176). This store[4] had been built in the 1830s. During the First World War years and the 1920s it served as the busy shoe shop of Jesse F. Humphrey, who carried a very complete stock of men's, women's, and children's shoes and boots. In later years, Morley Keegan's shoe store was located here.

Ferrah's Bakery (no.174) was a pleasant store to visit. William Ferrah was primarily a baker of bread, which was delivered daily to his customers by horse and van (later by "Ferrah's Bread Truck"). His regular bread was baked as two single loaves side by side in the same pan and was called a "large loaf." If less was wanted, the double loaf was pulled apart through the middle, and a "small loaf" handed to you. (The large loaf cost 10 cents, the small loaf 5 cents.) Mr. Ferrah's fresh Dutch loaf was mouth-watering. Although bread was certainly to be bought in the store, customers were more likely to be shopping there for the fine assortment of sugar cookies, ladyfingers,(then very much in demand), fresh light and dark fruit-cake, hot-cross buns (in Lent), or very fresh buns, with or without currants. The home-made candy was delicious: peanut-brittle, fudge, maple-cream, and a treat I often dream about, Ferrah's Turkish Delight. The back section of the store, separated by a trellis-like divider holding many kinds of fern and flanked by two enormous rubber-plants, was the ice-cream parlour. With its ice-cream tables and chairs, so popular now as antiques, and its decorative terrazzo flooring, this was an attractive and popular place, particularly on a hot summer day. Ferrah's ice cream, freshly made with real cream, needs a more poetic pen than mine to do it justice!

A small building with a rounded roof and metal siding, standing next to Ferrah's, was the downtown C.N. Express Office of Arthur Hillmer. Some years later it became the shoe-repair store of Art Butler, and subsequently the first "Opportunity Shop,"[5] operated during the Second World War by the Angela Bruce Chapter, I.O.D.E. (Of no further use, this small building has stood forlornly in recent years, on Cross Avenue opposite the Dominion Store parking-lot.) No.170 was the site of a large grocery and feed store established by Henry Wilson in 1871 and carried on after his death in 1908 by his son Gordon. Demolished in the 1920s, this fine store was replaced by a larger shop: Loblaw Groceteria, which remained in the same location until after the Second World War.

The southeast corner at Thomas Street was left vacant after the fire which destroyed Gulledge's Shoe Store there, and the area was partially hidden by a fence. However, in 1921-22 the handsome Bank of Toronto was built here. This bank had been located since 1902 in smaller quarters in the Anderson Building in the next block west. Mr. James B.L. Grout was manager in both old and new banks for a great number of years. In 1906 a corner-store on the other side of Thomas was remodelled and enlarged into a hotel, the Decker House, boasting a 52-foot bar. Ample hotel-space was needed in small towns then, largely because of the frequent visits of commercial travellers, upon whom the merchants were so dependent. These travelling salesmen used the railways from town to town to visit their customers for orders and sales, and usually had to stay over for a day or two in each town.

South of the Decker House, towards Robinson Street, ran the hotel's covered "drive-shed,"[6] typical of those years, for the accommodation of horse-drawn vehicles belonging to patrons of the hotel. On Sundays, however, Mr. Decker generously allowed his drive-shed to be used by church-goers to St. Jude's, who needed a place to tie up their horses and carriages during Morning Service. I vaguely remember my father making use of this convenience for a year or two — until we moved closer to town and he owned a motor car! In 1911 or 1912 this hotel changed hands and became for very many years the Gibson House, operated by the Gibson family; it is now the Halton Inn. The butcher shop of George MacDonald stood next to the hotel, but has long since been torn down for a customers' parking-lot for the Halton Inn.

In a white-stucco house close to the sidewalk (no.152), west of MacDonald's Butcher Shop, lived Mr. E.H. Gulledge as an older man. It was quite a surprise to find, in the middle of this business block, his little garden behind a picket fence and gate. His son Alan and family lived on Randall Street, east of the Radial Terminal at Thomas Street. The shop of William Whitaker Sr. (nos.144—46) was a busy place. Expert steam- and pipe-fitters, plumbers, and heating experts were employed here, and their services were always in demand. Most of the heavy work was carried out at the rear, approached from Robinson Street.

The grocery store of James L. Hewson (no.142) was, in a word, "first-class." It was referred to often by customers and others of that time as "the Michie's of Oakville" — high praise, indeed, since Michie's was the foremost purveyor of fine groceries in Toronto. Meticulous care was given always to filling the vast number of telephone orders which kept Mr. Hewson's delivery facilities operating at a non-stop pace. A truly fine grocery store, not to be forgotten.

The still handsome Anderson Building (nos. 134-38) was built to include the private bank of C.W. Anderson and Son. With the failure of the bank in 1902, Mr. Anderson lost this building to his creditors, as well as his large house and farm of some 200 acres, which in a few years became the "Brantwood Survey."[7] The old Bank of Toronto located its premises in no.134 from that date until 1921, when it moved to a new building at Thomas and Colborne streets.

A few years after the old Town Hall on Navy Street burned to the ground in 1911, the town offices moved into the Anderson Building. The office of the town clerk occupied the present no.138; the Police Department was located next door (no.136), and its quarters included temporary accommodation for a small number of "transients" and minor offenders. During this period the chief of police, sometimes with one assistant, kept law and order in an exemplary manner within the town limits of Oakville. From the early 1900s these busy officers were, in succession, chief constables Felan, McCleary, Sweet, and Kerr; among the assistants were constables Jack Barnes and, later, William Roser and others.

The *Record*, one of Oakville's three weekly newspapers, was published in a part of the Anderson Building for a number of years by its able editor, Mr. W.J. Fleuty. A very large room on the second floor of this building, with cloak-rooms and "facilities," was known as Anderson's Hall and was used extensively for meetings, including those of the town council, and for all manner of dances and entertainment. The building later came to be known as the McPherson Building and the hall as McPherson's Hall.

"Oddfellows Hall 1883" is marked on the gables of the equally handsome building adjoining on the west, at the corner of Navy Street (nos.126—32). The second floor of this building also had a large meeting-hall which was used extensively. The *Star* was published weekly in the east half of this building, both before and after the turn of the century, by Mr. Arthur S. Forster, a veteran newspaperman and one-tme Mayor of Oakville. He advertised his newspaper as follows:

$1.00 a Year in Advance"

"THE STAR contains all the local news of town and district carefully compiled by watchful correspondents. All fresh and accurate.... THE STAR runs serial stories constantly. Only those by the brightest and best authors published...."

The last store on the Main Street (no.126), but by no means the least, was the fine dry-goods store of the courtly Mr. Robert Barclay, who carried on his father's well-established business on the latter's death in 1900. In 1912 the following advertisement appeared locally:

"The R.B. BARCLAY BUSINESS to-day is a SPECIALIZED BUSINESS, being devoted to DRY GOODS, GENT'S FURNISHINGS and CLOTHING."

This shop later became the dry-goods store of Mr. W.E. McIlveen. It should be pointed out that, throughout this period, Oakville merchants were hard-pressed to compete with the large city stores, such as Eaton's, Simpson's, and Murray-Kay's in Toronto, which were always ready and willing to deliver their goods free of charge to Oakville consumers (in the early part of the century by rail, later by motor truck). The merchants, on the whole, should be congratulated upon keeping a very complete stock-in-hand for their customers. One heard on every side the slogan: "Buy in Oakville."

The four-storey brick Tannery building at the southwest corner of Navy Street was a conspicuous ending to the Main Street. A handsome general store built by Gage, Hagaman & Company in the 1860s, it had become part of the Marlatt and Armstrong Leather Company by the 1890s, and was used for processing fancy leathers for glove-making, purses, etc. For a time Wilbur T. Marlatt was in partnership here with Julian Sale, of the widely known Julian Sale Leather Company in Toronto. (It was indeed a "landmark fire"[8] that destroyed this building when it was owned by Mr. J.R. Kendall, also a manufacturer of fine leathers.)

West of this corner, towards the river, Oakville's original Post Office still stood where it had first been located in the 1830s. This small, old building became the nucleus of the Oakville Post Office Museum in the 1950s. But after its replacement in 1856 by Mr. Robert Balmer's "new" Post Office, built on the north side of Colborne Street (approximate present location, no.175), it had stood vacant for almost 100 years and served no particular purpose, though occasionally used for storage space. At the end of the 1920s, Mr. Percy Bath, by extending one end of the building, constructed inside it, entirely by hand, a cabin cruiser for himself. Having completely fitted up the boat for comfortable living, he spent many summers living aboard the *Psyche* and entertaining his family and friends on short cruises and picnics up the river and on the lake. This was the last useful purpose the old Post Office building served before it was moved to Lakeside Park and restored by Hazel Mathews as a repository for Chisholm, and other, artifacts of the early days.

NORTH SIDE

At the beginning of the Main Street on the north side was the Whitaker family property on the northwest corner of Colborne and Dundas streets. Since the late 1800s this property, extending from Colborne to Church Street, had accommodated the home and carriage business of Wm. Whitaker & Sons. Nearest to Church Street stood their busy blacksmith shop and next door their carriage shop, which later became a large garage and showroom for cars; both faced on Dundas Street. The Whitaker home was approached from Dundas Street, but was visible from the Main Street, over a long stretch of lawn reaching north to the house.

On the Whitaker property at the northwest corner of Dundas Miss Freestone's store did a thriving business in fish and chips, and, with the younger trade, in her home-made candy, particularly her sponge-taffy. After the First World War this corner-store was operated as a grocery by Mr. A. F. Hass. Electrical contractor B.E. Sprowl occupied the adjoining store and to the west lay the Whitakers' lawn mentioned above. Members of the Whitaker family were often to be seen sitting on their verandah watching the world go by on the Main Street, half a block away across their lawn. (This portion of the Main Street is difficult to identify, since the White Oak Centre now covers the northwest corner.)

The Oakville Garage (Robin and Bath) c.1912

The old building that is today nos.265—67 Lakeshore has occupied this site since 1887, when Knox Presbyterian Church was built at the southeast corner of Dunn Street. To make room for the new church, a large hotel, the White Oak, which had stood on the corner since before the 1850s, was divided into three parts and moved elsewhere. This building on the north side was one of the three, and had been moved across the street to its present position.[9] Here, in 1911, when the motor car showed signs of becoming the "thing of the future," my father and Mr. Percy Bath ventured into the automobile business, taking on the first Ford car agency in town. In 1912 a two-passenger Ford "runabout" could be bought for $675, a five-passenger "touring-car" for $750, and a six-passenger "town-car" — "a model of utility and beauty" — for $1,000. Robin and Bath also had the Reo agency. In 1913 the standard price for the Reo -- "fully equipped with electric self-starter" — was $1,750.

Set back from the street and west of the garage was "Sandy" MacDonald's busy blacksmith shop — with clanging hammer-on-anvil and the smell, which was pleasant (to me), of horses' hoofs being shod. A nice shaded piece of lawn came next, belonging to Mr. Joe Mitchell, who owned the grocery and feed store at the corner of Dunn Street (no.245). At this corner stood, outside Joe Mitchell's Grocery Store, a very handsome drinking-fountain, designed to provide a drinking-trough for horses, a trough at a lower level for dogs, and "founts of the latest type, requiring no cups, for human use." This fountain stood on the sidewalk at the edge of the road, to be available to all three, and was the generous gift — much appreciated by man and beast — of the Ladies Sunshine Circle.

Across Dunn Street was the long-established butcher shop of William A. Buckle (now the Royal Trust). To enter this shop was to step onto a thick carpet of clean sawdust, marked by the occasional pool of blood dripping from a whole hog or piglet hanging from the ceiling. The shop was festooned with carcasses dangling from hooks: whole sides of beef and I know not what else; fowl, of course, and in the proper season, turkeys. I grew bored in Buckle's while mother and Mr. Buckle dickered about the best cuts, since to me one carcass pretty much resembled another. But when Mr. Buckle finally stood at his huge chopping-block, wielding his meat-cleaver and other gory knives — *that* was entertainment! Buckle's was a fine, brick, two-storey building; living-quarters took up the west side and the second storey, while the butcher shop ran along the Dunn Street side, with windows facing on the Main Street as well as on Dunn.

A high board-fence effectively hid the Buckles' garden, and to the west were the steps leading up into Ben Walsh's (and later Mrs. Slean's) Grocery. Later still, this was a bookstore, owned at different times by Fred W. Grinham and Alex Guild. Several steps led also to Alex Shepherd's Tailoring and Dry-Cleaning Shop and, beside it, the small shop where Mrs. Lean carried Butterick patterns and other necessities for sewing.

The two-storey brick building that is now no.221 was built in 1910 by Mr. Louis V. Coté to accommodate Oakville's Fourth Post Office. Mr. Coté was postmaster from 1904 until his death in 1937. The east half of the ground-floor was fitted from floor to a reachable height with row after row of the townspeople's Post Office boxes, numbered and locked. The necessary wickets for stamps, parcels, and registered letters, were attended by young men and women who knew most of the box-holders and customers by sight. Should you happen to misplace your precious Post Office key, Mr. Coté, if he were in his usual good mood, would take the mail from your box and hand it to you through the wicket. The only thing that tried Mr. Coté's patience, as I remember, was children who roller-skated into the Post Office to pick up their mail — and who could blame him! "Picking up the mail" was a pleasant custom and added to the familiarity of the townspeople with one another, since they met frequently in the Post Office. Rural delivery looked after those out of town.

The west half of Mr. Coté's building was the drugstore of Frank N. Kyle. Hanging over the sidewalk, a long vertical sign announced: "FRANK N. KYLE — DRUGS 'N EVERYTHING." W.T. Weiland was the next to operate this drug store. The site, however, was always remembered affectionately in more recent years as the home of the fine drug store and soda fountain of the popular Len Hope. Space was designed on the second floor of the building for the Customs Office, where Captain Maurice Felan in the early 1900s and Mr. William Ferrah in the 1920s were the customs officers. C.M. Heddle's wool brokerage business also had quarters on the second floor.

Next to the Post Office building was the second location of McDermott's Barber Shop, later Bellman's Barber Shop with a pool hall in the rear. To the west was the first-class men's tailoring shop of A.A. Aiken, whose advertisement in a 1908 newspaper read:

> "WE SELL THE FORSYTHE SHIRT. BEST VALUE FOR $1.00.
> A,A. AIKEN, MERCHANT TAILOR, OAKVILLE."

In the same premises Joseph Carberry later conducted a fine tailoring business for some years. The present no.215, then as now a hardware store,[10] was owned and operated by the Coote family and, in the 1920s, by George W. Bailey. The three-storey, brick building next door (no.205) was built in the 1860s by Obadiah Marlatt, and for the greater part of the early 1900s was occupied by Francis B. Robinson, who lived with his family on the upper floors. On the ground floor Mr. Robinson carried a complete stock of dry goods — a fine store in every way, but smelling strongly of coal-gas.

W.H. Moore, with his sons, operated a hardware business at the northeast corner of George Street for many years, and later Fred W. Grinham moved his bookstore to this location. This is the present site of the Bank of Nova Scotia. Across George Street, the barber shop and pool hall of Charles Bradbury carried on an active business. He was succeeded by R.E. Knowles and finally by Frank Payne, the last barber to operate here. In front of the barber-shop at that time were large horse-chestnut trees, a "horse's-head" hitching-post, and, of course, a prominent red-and-white striped barber's pole. The family lived beside and above the shop, and their pretty garden was on the west.

The foregoing is a description of the corner prior to 1922. In that year Mr. W.S. Davis had the former Bradbury Barber Shop building moved in two sections to new locations on William Street. Here they were converted into houses, the rear section becoming a double house (nos.186—88 William) and the front section (no.225) a single dwelling. Mr. Davis then engaged Shaw Brothers of Oakville, builders and contractors, to erect a two-storey bank building on the corner of George Street. It housed the new branch of the Canadian Bank of Commerce, which in 1923 amalgamated with the Bank of Hamilton; Mr. E.M. Paynter, formerly an inspector with the Bank of Hamilton, became manager of this new branch. Mr. Davis' own large real estate office occupied the west portion of the new building, and later the United Suburban Gas Company was located here in his former office.

In the 1900s, hanging outside the next building (no.193) was a large, round, wooden sign, painted to resemble a clock, with the words "WILLIAM BUSBY, JEWELLER." (This sign is in the possession of the Oakville Historical Society.) Mr. Busby was also manager until 1912 of the Bell Telephone Company, whose switchboard and apparatus were set up at the back of his jewellery store. In 1909

William Busby, jeweller: store and residence

Oakville had 100 telephones; the number had doubled by 1911 and had increased to 500 in 1915, at which time the Exchange was moved to the second floor of a newly constructed two-storey, brick building next door (no.191). This building occupied the space that had formerly been the garden of the Busby family. In 1923 the Bell Telephone Exchange moved to a new and larger building at the northwest corner of Randall and Dundas Street.

Mr. Busby was a jeweller in the true sense of the word, and was usually to be seen at his work-table in the front window of the store, watchmaker's magnifying glass stuck in one eye, untiringly repairing a watch, clock, or piece of jewellery. The shop contained behind glass cases the usual stock of silverware (plated and otherwise), china, cut-glass articles, watches, clocks, and jewellery. On one of the counter-tops was a high stand stacked with picture postcards of Oakville. At the very back of the store stood a very large and beautiful grandfather clock, with a rather pronounced, deep "tick-tock" and chime. Mr. and Mrs. Busby were pillars of the Methodist Church. He served as chairman of the Oakville Board of Education for 25 years, and was its oldest member at the time of his death at 82.

On the street floor of the second Telephone Exchange building (no.191) was the candy store and ice-cream parlour of L.A. Wilkinson, where not only Neilson's ice cream and candy might be bought but,

Davis Block and Bank of Hamilton, 1914

more important, the delicious home-made candy produced by Mr. Wilkinson himself. In 1903 Mr. W.S. Davis built a fine brick building to the west (nos.185—89), in the east half of which he conducted his real estate business. For a few years Oakville's Third Post Office occupied the adjoining office in the west half. When the Post Office was moved to Mr. Louis Coté's new building one block east in 1910, the Bank of Hamilton opened a branch here (no.187) with Mr. Davis as manager, a position he held until 1923 when the Bank of Hamilton amalgamated with the Canadian Bank of Commerce. A stairway in this building led from the sidewalk to offices on the second floor; these included the law office of Mr. Alec Chisholm and the offices, in succession, of doctors Anderson, Duff, and Deans, all dentists. On the same floor a private school for girls was run for several years, first by Miss Willis and later by Miss Vera Crossley.

Down on the street level was John R. Byers' Drug Store,[11] known to so many for a great number of years. While I was a pupil at the private schools mentioned above, however, this drugstore was operated by Mr. Lorne Springstead. Before the Lunau Block (nos.179—83) housing E.P. Lunau's dry-goods store, was built in 1922, a small garden, hidden behind the customary board-fence, occupied the space[12] between Mr. Davis' and the next stores to the west. This garden served as a make-shift playground for the pupils of the private school located upstairs in the Davis Building, and a bonus for us was a more ample supply of apples than we could possibly eat, growing on a variety of very old trees there.

The store-fronts are so altered in the rest of this block that I will attempt only to name the shops; I cannot give exact locations or recall in what chronological order they followed one another. However, I remember the stores clearly: W.K. Leggatt, harness and leather store; Jack Meadows, "Quick Lunch"; Charlie Chung, Chinese laundry. Rather notable historically was Phoebe Baker's (no.171); this toy-shop was crammed with rather dusty relics of toys from another day, but still held irresistible attraction for children of all ages. In the 1920s George Green operated his barber shop here, with a pool room overhead, and, incidentally, undertook to cut and shampoo hair for the ladies. This was a distinct innovation in a men's barber shop! The long-established barber Dan McDermott was located next door (no.169) and was somewhat of a tradition on the Main Street.

In the general area of no.167 Lakeshore was located Messrs. Groves and Dixon's home-made candy shop, "The Paragon"; its spacious ice-cream parlour at the rear was a favourite meeting-place after the "show" and dances. The "Banana Split" was then, as now, a perennial favourite, but in a class by itself was their "Tin Roof" (ice cream smothered in chocolate sauce and topped off with peanuts). In this same block were situated, unbelievably side by side, branches of the Dominion Store and the A & P Food Store, managed respectively by Ross Litchfield and Russell Harris.

I am told that Gilleland's Barber Shop occupied the northeast corner of Thomas Street, but I remember only a branch of the United Cigar Stores there. It is interesting to realize that the large building at this corner once was the old Wesleyan Methodist Church, moved from the corner of Dunn and Randall streets to make way for the present St. John's Church, built there in 1878. The Merchants Bank, Oakville's first chartered bank (Mr. F.G. Oliver, manager), opened in 1898 at the northwest corner of Thomas Street in an old wooden building which, long before, had been the first St. Jude's Church and later, minus the steeple, the hardware store of Sam McGiffin. In 1910 the bank erected the brick building which is now occupied by the Bank of Montreal; for the greater part of our period its manager was Mr. H.L. (Lionel) Read, who lived with his family of four girls and three boys at no.215 William Street.

West of the bank the original roofs of two venerable small stores can still be seen (though barely) behind the "false fronts" on nos.155 and 149 Lakeshore. A watchmaker's shop, operated in the last century by "Zeke" (Ezekiel) Smith, was carried on by his widow and his son Wilbert until it closed in the 1930s; it was known up to the last as "Zeke Smith's." This same location (no.155) was popular for some years afterwards as a small Chinese restaurant owned by Lem Gooey. W.R. Wales — "Feed - Seeds - Groceries" — stood next door (no.149). Early in the century this store bore remains of the then popular style of a roof extending over the sidewalk, supported by posts. The three-storey brick building to the west (no.145)[13] in my memory was A. & G. Hillmer's large automobile showroom, which became a busy place as more and more families provided themselves with cars. This business was the final outcome of the famous Hillmer livery stables and all that the Hillmer family stood for in the name of "transportation."[14] Mr. Joe Ming, the next occupant, operated the Savoy Cafe here for a number of years.

Fire destroyed a group of shops west of the Hillmer building, including McDermott's original barber shop, their places soon being taken by new ones. Spared from the fire was the store directly east of the Oakville House (approximate present location, nos.131—35), in which Gerald P. Mitchell had published the *Oakville News* from 1907 until he moved to Dunn Street. Oakville, however, could not support three weekly newspapers, and Gerry Mitchell eventually moved to Hamilton. The fine meat market of Dymock and Leslie flourished in this location for some time, and the store was subsequently used for a number of businesses, one of which, not to be forgotten, was Leonard Cornwall's Insurance Office.

With the Oakville House[15] we come to the end of the Main Street. Much has been written about this historic hotel, which is said to be the oldest of its kind in Ontario to have continued in uninterrupted use as an hotel. In the period 1900—30 it had reached the stage of having seen better days.

Footnotes:

[1] In 1833 Mr. Justus W. Williams, father of Dr. J.S.W. Williams, became owner of the east half of the block between Dundas and Dunn and erected a frame-dwelling and shop on this location. (The reminiscences of another son, John Aikman Williams, were of great help to Hazel Mathews in writing *Oakville and The Sixteen).*

[2] Thomas Nisbet (1870—1928) was the son of the Reverend James Nisbet, first minister of the Canada Presbyterian Church in Oakville. Thomas, with his sister, Mrs. S. Bacon, and their family, lived for many years in "The Manse" (no.10 Park Avenue).

[3] Built by William Uptegrave in 1831. An ancient and historic "Exchange" for stage-coaches.

[4] It contained for some time the bakery and ovens of John and Robert Ferrah, father and son, who came from Scotland to Canada in 1854. Later, their new bakeshop and store, also living-quarters, of two-storey red brick were built next door (no.174).

[5] The "Opportunity Shop" was an outlet for the saleable articles collected during the stupendous war effort engaged in by I.O.D.E. members — the town-wide pick-up, sorting, and re-sale of "salvage" needed for war materials.

[6] Present location of the Department of National Defence.

[7] "Brantwood Survey": see p. 110.

[8] "Landmark fire": see p. 45.

[9] The second section may be seen as no.152 Lakeshore Road; the third section, occupied in our time by Mr. A.E. Gibson and his family, is no.350 King Street.

[10] William Creighton, who came from Ireland, established a general store in this building in the late 1830s.

[11] Mrs. Dorothy (Byers) Sutton has donated to the Oakville Historical Society valued photographs of some of the contents of her father's drugstore; many of these items were given to Mr. Byers by Dr. Urquhart when he gave up his own drugstore.
[12] Oakville's Second Post Office (Mr. Robert Balmer, postmaster) was located here from 1856 to 1903, when the Third Post Office was opened next door in a new building erected by Mr. W.S. Davis in 1903. Mr. Balmer then "about-faced" his old Post Office building, placing it on Church Street, where it remained as a double house until the 1960s. Hence the "space" left on Colborne Street for some 20 years, until the erection of Mr. E.P. Lunau's building.
[13] Built by James Reid in 1853. Among many owners before our time were William Hixon Young, cabinet-maker, undertaker, and post-master, and W.G. Hewson, grocer and father of James L. Hewson (see p. 130).
[14] For the Hillmer family and transportation, see pp. 47-55.
[15] Although William Chisholm was the initial owner of Oakville's first hotel in 1829, William J. Sumner, a close friend from their Wellington Square (Burlington) days, at first leased, and in 1834 bought, the hotel. (Here in 1831 the first Public Auction of town lots had taken place.) William Sumner added a third storey in 1867; John Williams was one of a long line of proprietors.

"Psyche"

The Town Hall (1863-1911) (site: north of present Bowling Green)

10
Navy Street

William Chisholm had selected the site of Oakville because of its suitability as a lake port, and it followed that Navy Street,[1] leading to and from the harbour, was a very busy thoroughfare in his time. It continued to be so throughout the 1800s, since all supplies for the town arrived by ship, and all the products of the region — grain, flour, and fruit — were transported from here to other ports in this way. Along the river's edge at the ends of Robinson, William, and King streets, stood large warehouses and granaries. Horses with wagons plodded down these hills to unload their goods, and coal, ice, gravel, and provisions for the town were carried up to Navy Street from the riverside in the same way. Fresh fruit to be shipped was carted down the hill (south of "Erchless") to the harbour and unloaded into a shelter on the north end of the pier, built for protection from the sun and weather.

All this activity explains the presence in the 1800s of two large hotels on Navy Street: Frontier House on the southeast corner of Navy and King streets, and the Canadian Hotel at the southeast corner of Navy and Robinson. In the 1900s, with Murray Williams as the proprietor, the name of the latter was changed to the Murray House. Navy Street was also the obvious location in 1862 for the Town Hall, incorporating market building, auditorium, council chambers, and Lock-up. The hall stood north of the present Bowling Green until destroyed by fire in 1911. The Customs House took up a prime location near the harbour.

Two shoemakers' establishments were kept busy on Navy Street in the early days: William Sherburne's original house and workshop stood, until demolition in the 1960s, on the southwest corner of

Robinson Street, and on the northwest corner were the partners Kenney and Howes. In the 1900s, however, Dr. Dorland practised dentistry in the latter house, and, in my memory, it was the home of the Curran family for several years. The demolition, after more than 100 years, of this fine old brick house, with garden sloping down the steep hill on Robinson Street above the stone Granary, was one of the first of the losses sustained in the cause of "Park 16." An impressive, four-storey, brick building facing Navy Street at the southwest corner of Colborne Street (Lakeshore Road) built in the 1860s by Gage and Hagaman, general merchants, was in the first quarter of the 1900s a part of the Marlatt and Armstrong Leather Company. It has already been referred to as a landmark at the west end of "The Main Street," and it remained so until 1948, when destroyed by fire.

Home of R.K. Chisholm and Customs House (1850s)

The Chisholm property, the farthest block south on Navy Street on the west side, was concealed by a high brick wall. It was not then commonly spoken of as Erchless by the townspeople, but most certainly this part of Navy Street was enhanced by the estate and by the Customs House that stood on the corner of the property. In the mid-1850s Mr. R.K. Chisholm had built both the Customs House and the part of Erchless standing beside it and overlooking the lake. During the early 1900s, after Mr. Chisholm's death in 1899, Erchless was occupied by his widow, son Allan, and daughter, Mrs. Parrish, and her two daughters. Later it was leased and occupied at different times by J.H. Gundy, the Scotts, and A.P. Turner. From the 1920s Mrs. John A. Chisholm and her daughters Hazel and Juliet were occupying Erchless, the Customs House, and the renovated carriage-house on King Street.

Mr. and Mrs. John Chisholm were residents of New York State, and in the 1890s they built a beautiful and spacious Oakville home, "Mount Vernon," in which they and their daughters spent the summer months. This three-storey, clapboard house of attractive architecture, painted a delicate yellow with white trim, looked out over Lakeside Park towards the water, and the stables and gardens ran north behind the house as far as King Street. After Mr. Chisholm's death early in the

"Mount Vernon", once home of John A. Chisholm, Lakeside Park. (destroyed by fire 1928)

1900s, the house was occupied by a series of tenants until 1928, when it tragically burned to the ground. This was a great loss, not only to the Chisholm family but to the beauty of that part of town. The site formerly occupied by Mount Vernon, however, provided extra space in Lakeside Park, enjoyed by the citizens for its position on the lakefront, its bandstand, and its pair of large cannon, placed there when the park was first formed in the 1800s. These cannon held great attraction for the public and for the children playing in the park, but they were finally melted down for their metal content during the Second World War.

Most readers are likely to have learned something of the historic hotel Frontier House, which stood on the southeast corner of Navy and King streets in the 1800s but which was later divided and formed into two houses. Since our period runs from 1900 to 1930, we are concerned here only with the family of Mr. Robert Swanton Appelbe, which occupied the house that remained on this corner[2] from 1870 until some 70 years later. Much of historic interest is known of the Appelbe family, and it would be time well spent to read of it in Hazel Mathews' *Oakville and The Sixteen*. However, the memories shared by a great many who were children in the first and second decades of the 1900s and who were lucky enough to have learned to play the piano from an expert teacher, Miss Kathleen Appelbe, are those which long remain. Miss Appelbe was a perfectionist, an excellent performer on the piano herself, and she somehow managed to remain serene throughout the sometimes agonizing attempts by some of her pupils in a musical direction. The piano ranked high in importance and was a source of pleasure in most families of that era, and I myself have always been grateful to "Miss Appelbe" for contributing to my lifelong enjoyment of it.

Home of Family of R.S. Appelbe (1870-1940s)

Captains Robert and William Wilson lived, until the early 1860s, in the two houses north of King Street. Needless to say, these old houses have enjoyed a long succession of owners since that time. In the early 1900s Mrs. Pullen, widow of Captain Hugh F. Pullen, occupied the present no.41 Navy Street. I well remember Mr. and Mrs. Bertram Tate, who later lived in this house with their family, Bertram Junior (known as "June"), Frank, Alf, and Serena; the children all did their part in livening up the neighbourhood. In the 1920s Miss Marion Sanders and her niece had their home there. The family of Mr. Nelson King lived at this time in the next house to the north (no.45).

W.S. Davis, in the early years of his illustrious career in the town, lived on the southeast corner of William Street. Here began his family of five fine sons. Mr. and Mrs. Charles Cox and Dorothy lived here next, followed by Mr. and Mrs. Mahoney (first syllable accented), Ed and Nora. In the 1830s, Mr. William J. Sumner[3] built two houses at right angles to one another at the northeast corner of William and Navy Streets. The one facing Navy Street (no.65) was occupied, in my memory, by the family of the prominent Oakville plumber Mr. Fred Millison, while around the corner at no.145 William Street lived Colonel Walter Moorhouse and his family. In 1855 William J. Sumner's son, George,[4] had moved into the William Street house, and

"The Sumner Home, 1833" (145 William Street)

members of the Sumner family resided there continuously until the 1920s, when the house was bought by Colonel Moorhouse; it still remains in his family.

Walter Moorhouse, as an architect, took great pains in his restoration to leave the exterior of this 1833 house as unchanged as possible, and the interior is equally charming. It stands today complete with its hitching-post, an excellent illustration of the fact that such historic treasures need not suffer the mutilation so often inflicted upon them. (I have deviated slightly from the "straight and narrow" up Navy Street, turning these few feet east on William Street in order to pay a tribute to Walter Moorhouse, without whose untiring interest, research, photographic record of old Oakville houses and buildings, and general architectural expertise Oakville, as well as the Oakville Historical Society, would be the poorer today.)

Those passing the hotel garden lying south of the Murray House frequently stopped to enjoy watching an ornate fountain, in which the water, flowing out and over the top, kept a ball perpetually dancing in mid-air. The proprietor of the Murray House, Mr. Murray Williams, was another who laid claim to having owned the first motor car in Oakville! The corner house north of the Murray House (no.85 Navy) was built in the 1850s by Oakville's first Mayor, Colonel George K. Chisholm, a son of William Chisholm, the town's founder. Colonel Chisholm occupied the house for only a few years before building "The Retreat," which stood on lovely grounds near the west river-bank; this residence subsequently became the home and property of the Forster family until it fell victim to the present apartment buildings (no.199 Queen Mary Drive). Captain Maurice Fitzgerald and his descendants have occupied the corner house during the greater part of the 20th century. When we were children, this fine house took a place in our attention second only to the welcome sight of the picturesque Captain Fitzgerald, seated daily on his verandah, sporting a flowing beard and wearing his naval cap — a reminder of his long years as a captain on the Great Lakes. Most of us were too shy to go up and speak to him but many did, including the more "outgoing" Tate children, mentioned earlier! Descendants of Captain Fitzgerald still live in this delightful home and their preservation of it gives pleasure to all who pass by.

The pretty bungalow on the northwest corner of William and Navy streets was, for a time, the home of Colonel and Mrs. Windeyer and their daughter and son, Peggy and Dick. Chief Constable McCleary and Mr. T.C. Hagaman occupied the double house to the north (no.68 Navy Street). The old Sherburne home was still standing then at the southwest corner of Robinson Street, and next door Miss

MacLean operated one of many busy millinery shops in town. Hats were important in the early 1900s and a "Sunday-go-to-meeting" hat as well as a "second-best," for both summer and winter, were necessities. "Elaborate" is rather inadequate to describe some of these creations, decorated as they often were with feathers, flowers, fruit, and/or ribbon. The hats were generally made to order and many milliners were employed the year round.

Continuing north on Navy Street, one crossed Colborne Street (Lakeshore Road) to find the large expanse of the Central School playground (or "common"),[5] which lay between Navy Street and the creek bank; the school building itself stood at the north end of the common near Randall Street (the site partially occupied by the Centre of the Arts).The School Common was ideally and centrally situated for a variety of uses in the summer months. Carnivals, small Fairs, Garden Parties, and Rallies of all sorts took place here; it was useful, too, as a gathering-place to form up for the many parades which were popular then. One large event staged here took place in 1918 to celebrate the end of the First World War. The whole downtown was given over to the festivities, which included dancing for hundreds of happy people on the recently paved Main Street and which culminated in a mammoth bonfire, the purpose of which, I suspect, was burning the Kaiser in effigy. The wood for this huge bonfire was my father's donation of the "snake-fence" that bordered his property along the east side of Gloucester Avenue, from MacDonald Road to Sheddon.

Passing the school building on Navy Street, and crossing the Radial Car track over Randall Street,[6] one noticed a rather ancient building erected as a Methodist Episcopal Church in the 1860s. For a few years between 1910 and 1920 this building was used as a Kindergarten in connection with the Central School across Randall Street, and presided over by Miss "Kit" Elliot. The building was demolished in the 1960s. To the west of this building, near the creek bank and completely dominating the scene, stood the round, black stand-pipe used as a holding-tank for a reserve of town water, which was pumped up from the reservoir at the foot of Kerr Street. Children attending Central School looked forward to the thrilling sight of the occasional overflowing of this pipe, the result, perhaps, of some misjudgment at the Pumping Station. This might happen several times a year, and even the most blasé in the class were caught up in the excitement of watching the water cascading down the sides of the 100-foot stand-pipe. The present Fire Hall now occupies this northwest corner. I am told by my reliable authority on things pertaining both to fire-fighting and to the town itself, former Fire Chief Douglas Wilson, that the tremendous concrete foundation which had been necessary to hold the great weight of stand-pipe and water created a problem for contractors when they erected the present Fire Hall.

The farm of Mr. Edward Hillmer, on which grew orchards and other farm produce, had occupied a good part of the north end of Navy Street. There were a few neat houses, with small gardens, fences, and gates, on either side of this section of Navy and other nearby streets; these were said, in the 1800s, to be located in "French Village," since they were then occupied mainly by the families of the French shipwrights who worked in the yards in the nearby harbour. An apartment building and the Red Cross headquarters on the east side of Navy Street stand now on the site of some of these houses. A corner house, facing Randall Street, was the home of James Boocock, mentioned earlier as caretaker of the Public School.

"Hillmer's Paddock," contained by a high board-fence, occupied the northwest quarter of the block between Randall and Church Street (the present Oakville Plaza). It was used in conjunction with the Hillmer livery stable on the south side of Church Street (now the Legion Hall parking-lot). The paddock was also occasionally used enthusiastically by young baseball players. At the corner of Church Street, immediately south of the paddock, stood an attractive house of white stucco, the home of one-time Mayor of Oakville George Hillmer and Mrs. Hillmer, Charles, Arthur, Whitney, and Helen. This family played a prominent part in Oakville, as did that of Mr. Hillmer's brother Alfred, who, with Mrs. Hillmer, Blanche, Mary, Allan, and Bob, lived one house east on Church Street. (see Chapter 4)

Past the Legion Hall corner stood, as it does today, the old Oakville House Hotel, its service entrances and well-patronized bar facing Navy Street. In the main lobby of the hotel, facing Colborne Street, "Dickie" Smith operated a snack counter, popular with many, including school children who passed to and fro each day. This was the only store on the Main Street which I never entered, and I envied all those children who did. (It had been made clear to some of us that it was "quite unsuitable" for little girls to enter a hotel on their own — even if only for an ice-cream cone!)

Footnotes

[1] The British Navy was high in everyone's regard in the 1830s, particularly in Oakville where ships, sailors, and shipbuilding predominated.

[2] The other half of Frontier House was moved around the corner, east along King Street (no.154), to become the home of Mr. Charles Phillips.
[3] William Johnson Sumner: owner and proprietor in the 1800s of the Oakville House Hotel.
[4] George Johnson Sumner (1834-1911) filled, during the course of his lifetime, almost every official post in town. Besides holding the exacting position of Chief Constable, he was Tax Collector, Health and Truant Officer, and Harbour Master, was in complete charge of the Town Hall and Lock-up, and occasionally assisted the undertaker, George Ziller, in laying out the dead. Fortunately for posterity, Constable George Sumner kept diaries, written with his own dry humour, of his daily round of tasks and, through the kindness of the George Doty family, these diaries were made available to Hazel Mathews, enabling her to give an accurate account of the happenings of that period in Oakville's history in *Oakville and The Sixteen*. (These irreplaceable diaries have been generously donated recently to the Oakville Historical Society by Joan (Doty) Havill, a great grand daughter.)
[5] The school "common" or playground: the space now occupied by the Centennial complex on Navy Street.
[6] Randall Street: in the 1950s, through a typographical error in ordering street signs for the town, the final "l" was omitted from the word Randall, the mis-spelled signs, "Randal Street," offending the eye at each intersection on that street. This seemed to me an affront to that gentleman's memory, and I engaged in a running battle with those responsible for the error. The proof of spelling was easily to be found in Jacob Randall's own firm signature, appearing in deed books at Milton's County Registry Office. Eventually new signs appeared, this time correctly spelled "Randall Street," commemorating this fine gentleman, a noted shipbuilder and owner of Oakville's original Town Lot Number I, for whom William Chisholm named the street running through this property. (At the same time corner signs on Park Avenue suddenly appeared spelled "Parke." It was easily verified that, until the Carson development in the early 1900s, this street was merely a path running along a wooded section to the Nisbet and Bacon home (no.10 Park Avenue) and leading to Orchard Park, for which the avenue was named. The signs eventually re-appeared as "Park Avenue.") How easily neglect of a little research in these matters can render historical names quite meaningless.

A Dance in Victoria Hall, 1914

11
Recreation 1900-1930

The subject of recreation in the first 30 years of the 1900s is very unlikely to catch the interest of people of today, whose every waking moment is occupied by television, radio, movies, theatre, discos, snowmobiles in Winter, and fast cars and boats in Summer. If any thought were given to the subject, it would be to reflect that life must, indeed, have been *boring* in those days, when none of the above was available. Instead, the opposite was the case. In a small town of Oakville's size, the difficulty often was to choose among several activities taking place at the same time, whether in the line of sports, active or spectator, some social event, large or small, or in a succession of "entertainments," which followed one another fairly closely during the course of the year.

Because we lacked the continuous, "mechanical" sources of entertainment of the present, anything which came our way, such as a movie, concert, play, or musical performance, easily caught and held our interest and usually made for our enjoyment. Generally speaking, there was something in this line to look forward to, either in the Hall or in one of the churches or schools. You could say that we were easily pleased — naïve if you like — but in spite of, or perhaps because of this, we led very happy lives.

THE HALL

The old Town Hall stood until 1911 on Navy Street, north of the present Bowling Green, and the second floor with its stage and fairly large seating capacity was the centre for amusements in the town; every conceivable concert and performance is said to have taken place there. An Oakville newspaper of 1908 describes the showing of an early movie:

> "A good-sized audience witnessed the moving picture show in the town hall last Monday evening. The scenes were good and clear. . . .The Company will show more pictures in the near future, 'accompanied by singing'(!)"

One wide, wooden staircase to the second floor provided the sole entrance and exit and, since the entire building was constructed of wood, it was considered to be a mercy that there was no loss of life when the Town Hall burned down in 1911. Many happy times had been spent there by one and all for the best part of 50 years.

Taking the place, after the fire, of the old Town Hall as the centre for year-round entertainment was Victoria Hall on Reynolds Street (now the Curling Club parking-lot). This was a hall to be proud of and was well designed, with a fine stage and dressing-rooms; two slightly raised galleries running the full length of the Hall on both sides, provided a good view (along the lines of box-seats) of either stage or dance-floor, as the case might be. The large dance-floor of hardwood was often described as "smooth as glass." In the 1920s the new up-to-date Gregory Theatre[5] (now the Canada Trust corner) pretty well replaced Victoria Hall for stage productions, imported as well as local, and moving pictures.

Frequently from Toronto or elsewhere came productions of drama or comedy, as well as musicians, hypnotists, and other entertainers; these performances were well attended. Drawing a similarly full house were the many concerts, plays, and Glee Club and Choral Society performances by our own good local talent. The Oakville men enjoyed putting on a black-face minstrel show, complete with "end-men" and overflowing with jokes aimed at town celebrities and local situations. These always "brought the house down."

Townspeople were, then, well entertained by both local and visiting talent. However, it was a regular practice of the many who enjoyed the fine stage and musical productions available in Toronto to take advantage of the good train service between the city and Oakville. This frequent service gave theatre-goers easy access to hearing and seeing the world's best musical performers[1] at Massey Hall, top plays and musical comedies[2] from Broadway and other centres at the Royal Alexandra, the Princess,[3] and the Grand,[4] and vaudeville at Shea's

Hippodrome and Lowes' Theatre and Winter Garden. Following the paving in 1915 of the Lakeshore Road from Toronto, Lakeshore buses and private cars were used as well as the trains, which for many years beyond 1930 continued their excellent service.

MOVING PICTURES

Moving pictures in Victoria Hall pretty well looked after Saturday afternoons for every child in town — provided he had the five cents. Mr. Bertram Tate was the chief operator of this magical phenomenon. Wisely, the projection-room was located entirely outside the building and had to be approached by an outside staircase. Seating, being necessarily removable, was rather basic, consisting of row behind row of "kitchen-chairs," held in line by long planks running under them to form the rows. The good hardwood floor was covered with sawdust on these occasions for protection.

Fairly frequently the film would break or come to the end of a reel, and poor Mr. Tate would have to flash his sign: "Five Minutes, Please, to Change the Film." At this point, amid groans from the audience, the pianist who accompanied each movie non-stop would make an extra effort to calm our impatience. We emerged finally, screaming with laughter over Harold Lloyd, Charlie Chaplin, Fatty Arbuckle, Laurel and Hardy, Ned Sparks, Buster Keaton, or the Keystone Cops, but sometimes moved to sadness by tear-jerkers such as "Hearts of the World" with Dorothy and Lillian Gish or "Seventh Heaven" with Janet Gaynor. A few early favourites were Mary Pickford, Mary Miles Minter, Theda Bara in "The Vamp," Gloria Swanson, Mabel Normand, and such "heroes" as Rudolph Valentino, Richard Barthelmess, William S. Hart, and Francis X. Bushman. Movie stars of the 1920s included John, Lionel, and Ethel Barrymore, George Arliss, Clara Bow (the "It" girl), Leslie Howard, Jeanette MacDonald and Nelson Eddy, Lawrence Tibbett, with his beautiful baritone voice, and Wallace Beery and Marie Dressler in "Tugboat Annie" and "Min and Bill." The list is endless. Among other excellent films produced in the 1920s were "The Four Horsemen of the Apocalypse," "Intolerance," and "Disraeli," starring George Arliss.

Pianists were in demand in small movie theatres to set the mood and match the caption on the screen. Snatches from "The Light Cavalry Overture" and similar lively tunes were used to accompany "action" on the film; "Hearts and Flowers" was a favourite for courting and love scenes. Large theatres had more scope. Some had an organ — possibly the popular Wurlitzer, which brought forth sounds of marching bands, blood and thunder, and mayhem, but which was able equally well to dissolve the audience in tears by use of the "tremolo," with sweet music. Orchestras, large and small, also earned good money accompanying the silent movie.

In the early 1920s the radio craze caught on, actually affecting attendance at the movies. Warner Brothers, to overcome this, adopted the newly perfected amplifier, which provided its own synchronized sound effect, and symphony music played along with the movie. In 1925 Fox Films introduced the use of the voice, through its popular "Fox News," and before 1930 the voice on synchronized sound disc brought an end to the silent movie.

DANCES

Large formal dances were held on the fine dance-floor of Victoria Hall. These might be put on as an annual, or special, affair by organizations such as the I.O.D.E. or the service clubs and by many other groups. During and after the First World War a large formal dance or "ball" was an extremely popular and successful way of raising money for the Red Cross, the Patriotic League, and similar public-spirited organizations.

Many families lived then in quite spacious houses, which lent themselves readily and frequently to large dancing-parties for boys and girls — young and not-so-young, as the case might be. All came dressed in their best party dresses or suits and, importantly, were greeted at the door by their hostess and host, who at the end of the party were on hand also to see that everyone was escorted home! This gave us the opportunity, as had been drilled into us at home, to say what a nice time we'd had. Fortunately, it was generally the truth! Who would not enjoy a vast expanse of hardwood floor and an excellent pianist or good "Jazz" records (or their equivalent!), with a mouth-watering "supper" half-way through the evening? Some of the more formal affairs used dance programmes (fox-trot, one-step, waltz, Paul Jones, etc.). These caused rather a flurry at the beginning of the party, because there was always the danger of the *wrong* boy writing himself on your programme for too many dances — or, horrors, for the "supper-dance" or "last dance" (despair!).

There were many smaller dances too, and less formal. "Mother and Dad," although not much in evidence, were always known "to be there." In the days when no home would have been complete without a piano, it followed naturally that there would always be at least one or two in a group who could be counted on to play for a few dances, as a change from the "Gramophone" or "Victrola." Ideally, too, someone would play the piano while everyone gathered round requesting favourite songs, one after another, and all joined in at the top of their lungs. Friday-night dances at the High School were popular also.

OAKVILLE CLUB

Originally a riverside granary and warehouse at the foot of William Street, the Oakville Club was formed in 1908 from a previously established Aquatic Club which had been used only in summer as a place for members to keep their boats. After it was renovated and made into a comfortable year-round club, members were always assured, even during the winter, of a place to meet friends. Saturday-night dances, as well as those for special occasions, on New Year's Eve and other celebrations, were very popular. In summer, dances on Saturday nights were considerably augmented by the crews of visiting yachtsmen from the Royal Canadian Yacht Club. The dance-floor was also packed when the Club entertained visiting tennis and badminton teams from other clubs.

Under the guidance initially of Norma (Mrs. James) Gairdner,[6] keen amateur actors and actresses at the Club produced stage plays year after year, in great variety, to enthusiastic audiences. These were followed in a few years by the ever-popular "Cabaret." In the early years of the Club, the bowling lanes on the ground floor were made good use of, until the addition of the badminton courts, when the space was needed for dressing-rooms and for access to the courts.

(There was no licence for a bar at the Oakville Club during the period we are covering; in fact, much of the time in my memory was governed by prohibition. This circumstance required a certain amount of "ingenuity" but, even so, "a good time was had by all!")

THE MONDAY CLUB

Many of the ladies of the town whiled away their time playing Bridge or sipping endless cups of tea with one another, which could not be called very stimulating recreation. To combat this, through the kindness of Mrs. C.P. Chisholm[7] the large "gallery," or north wing, of her home on Dundas Street (no.164 Trafalgar) was thrown open to members of the Monday Club for their afternoon meetings. This was a literary and cultural club for a large group of ladies who met to discuss the arts in the broadest sense of the word.

Each member took her turn in preparing and reading aloud a paper on an allotted subject related to the arts, mainly contemporary. These presentations might touch on Canadian or international artists, sculptors, architects, authors, or poets, the stage (comedy and tragedy), or other similar subjects. Programmes for these meetings were printed for each member in the form of a small booklet in the Club's colours: green and gold cover with gold-coloured pages. Usually the afternoon included a short musical programme, and tea, of course, was served. The Monday Club had a large and rather exclusive membership and continued for a number of years.

BOY SCOUTS AND GIRL GUIDES

In a small town such as Oakville the formation of the Boy Scouts and Girl Guide movements was of great benefit to the boys and girls of our period. A Boy Scout troop was formed in Oakville in 1911 under the leadership of Mr. Frank Chisholm. He was joined by Mr. John Cowan, a resident of Oakville who had had military and Scouting experience in Scotland, and they soon trained one of the best Scout troops in the Country. Very soon they had their own bugle band, trained by Mr. W.H. Tuck, bandmaster of the Oakville Band. Fine leaders, such as Tom Andrew, Alec Phillips, and others contributed greatly to Scouting in Oakville.

The Girl Guide movement did not take hold quite as readily as the Boy Scouts, although formed only a short time later. However, the Guides gradually built up a strong organization in Oakville under such leaders as Gladys Morgan, Faith Chisholm, and later Ruth Lightbourn and Mary Busby, to name only a few. The Guides enjoyed a summer camp, held regularly east of the town. In the early days of the movement we once boarded a special train and journeyed to Toronto to attend a rally of Girl Guides from all over Canada. This took place at the then unfinished "castle" of Sir Henry and Lady Pellatt, Casa Loma.

OAKVILLE SPORTS

"Whit" Hillmer, always considered one of Oakville's most

distinguished athletes, recalls the year-round interest in sports in the town:

"Having been born (1898) and raised in Oakville, I can seriously say that early in life I became aware of the fact that Oakville was one of the best sports-minded towns (2,500 population) in Ontario, with baseball and hockey being the most popular. Other sports had their place in the community, but not to the degree of spectator attendance that baseball or hockey enjoyed.

"My early life, as I recall it, was one of almost hero worhsip for the Baseball Team of that era, who played all their games in the old Oakville Fair Grounds on Reynolds Street. In the years just before the First World War most of our own baseball was played on Hillmer's lot, Randall and Navy streets, and the School Common, where the only Oakville Public and High Schools were located. Some of the older players became members of the Seniors at the Fair Grounds.

"Following the First World War a tremendous interest was created in both baseball and hockey by the development of a regulation baseball diamond and the building of a hockey-playing and skating arena. The baseball diamond was one of the best amateur playing-fields in Ontario. These developments were the fulfilment of the dreams of four sports-minded individuals: Arthur Hillmer Sr., Dave Chapman (later the manager of the Baseball Team), Wilbur Marlatt, and Charlie Hillmer. Spearheaded by these community-minded men, the whole town became involved. Out of these two developments at Victoria Park was born an athletic complex (to be known later as Wallace Park), consisting of ball park, hockey and skating rink, football field, lacrosse field, tennis-courts, and large community hall* with banquet facilities.

" In this ball park some of the best baseball in Ontario was played with teams from Toronto (Hillcrests, St. Andrews, St. Mary's, Oslers, and others). Hamilton teams included International Harvesters, Grand Trunks, Steel Company, etc.; teams also came from Bronte, Burlington, Milton, Acton, Georgetown, Campbellville, Brantford, Galt, Guelph, and St. Thomas, to mention just a few places. As a climax to our baseball enthusiasm and interest the town won the Intermediate Championship of Ontario in 1924.

"The community interest in baseball was carried over to hockey, which would play to 1,500 people at nearly every game. Hockey had its beginning on the Sixteen Mile Creek when Winter set in; those interested would, if wishing to play, make their own rinks by shovelling

* Victoria Hall

off the snow. Quite often the results of our efforts would be taken over by our seniors, much to our disgust, and we would move to another area and once again make our own rinks. The Sixteen, reaching from the Oakville Club, near the piers at the lake, up to the old grist mill (Ashbury's), near the railway tracks, made for beautiful skating and when clear of snow was well patronized. Skating parties on a moonlit evening were a beauty to behold, with everyone from the town able to skate taking advantage of the freeze-up. Soon we were to have rinks and hockey cushions on the 'Public School Marsh' as well as across the creek on the 'Tannery Marsh.'

"Then came the First World War, the war to end all wars, for which most young fellows, like myself, as well as the older ones volunteered. We who survived and were returned home in 1919 were pleasantly surprised at the local interest in sports as referred to in my previous remarks about baseball.

"The competition in the Halton County Hockey League was extremely keen, comprised as it was of teams from Burlington, Milton, Acton, Georgetown, and Oakville, who were the first champions in 1921—22. In later years (1934), strengthened by imports, we (Oakville) became the Intermediate Champions of Ontario. "Mac" McCleary was manager and Whit Hillmer his assistant. The team coach was Dr. F.M. Deans.

"To a somewhat lesser degree in popularity, soccer, cricket, lacrosse, Rugby football, and several other sports activities were engaged in at the community level. Other popular sports events were sailing races between the yacht clubs in Toronto and from Hamilton to Oakville on a time basis, held at least once a month during the season. A popular entry, and usually her class winner, was the Oakville yacht *Aggie*, owned by and sailed under the command of Mr. C. G. Marlatt, of the Marlatt and Armstrong Tannery, Oakville's largest industry of this period. Mr. Marlatt became the Commodore of the Royal Canadian Yacht Club of Toronto. Other water-sports events were the Sea Flea races held off Lakeside Park and usually won by a Toronto fleet under the supervision of Lou Marsh, the popular sports editor of the *Toronto Daily Star*. These events were followed on Saturday evenings by an always popular band concert under the direction of Mr. W.H. Tuck.

"I am sure all residents were agreed that the greatest and most enjoyable single-day sports event was the one held either on the First of July or on Civic Holiday, when the morning was taken up by water sports at the pier (east and west side). There were swimming races between the piers, distance races on The Sixteen between the Radial

Water Sports on "The Sixteen"

Bridge and the pier, canoe races, canoe tilting events, walking the greasy pole, dinghy races, and other water events. In the afternoon at the old Fair Grounds there would be baseball, jumping events, distance running and sprints, high jumping, broad jumping, shot putting, and other field events. An extremely happy, yearly event, attended as well by hundreds of 'out-of-towners.'

"Tennis became quite popular, particularly at the Oakville Club. This, I think, was the result of Sir Frank Baillie's invitation to several of the Davis Cup players to visit at his Lakeshore West estate as his guests and, on his new clay courts, to give exhibition matches for invited friends. Another recreational sport, mainly for the older citizens, was lawn bowling on the beautiful greens at their club on Navy Street.

"In concluding my reflections on sports activities in Oakville I would be remiss if the 'sport of kings' were not mentioned. Located at the eastern outskirts of Oakville, on the Lakeshore Road, was the famous farm of Mr. Harry Giddings, owner and operator, with his son Harry Jr., of one of the best-known breeding and training horse farms in North America. His horses, together with others, came under the training and racing directions of Harry Jr. The most famous and best remembered were the King's Plate winners he owned or trained for other sportsmen.

"The sports activities and events that I have recorded above are quite vivid in my mind and carry me back to the good old days in what to me was the best town in Ontario — Oakville."

HOCKEY

Winter sports were very popular in Oakville. Robert M. Chapman remembers the interest in hockey:

"The Oakville Athletic Association was an extremely keen and enterprising sports organization and was responsible, in 1920, for building the new indoor rink on the site of the present-day Curling Club. 'The New Rink', as it was called then, was erected with free help and contained a regulation hockey surface, as well as four lanes for curling along the sides of the rink. The New Rink was operated by an ice-maker, and the rest of the help was volunteer. 'Rink rats' was the nickname given to those who had the arduous task of keeping the ice scraped clean, between hockey periods and also during a long afternoon or evening of public skating, and who performed other jobs about the place. Without these boys, skating would have been difficult, or impossible. Mr. Ted Burrell, who was the builder, worked entirely gratis, and it is a tribute to his work that the same basic building, with understandable repairs, improvements, and additions, is still in use today 60 years later.

"The Oakville Hockey Team, who were Champions of Halton County in 1921 and 1922, are listed below in a salute to those fine hockey-players and their management who did honour to Oakville, both before and after the years mentioned:

Dr. F.M. Deans, Manager
Ollie Johnson, Trainer
Jack Osborne, L. Wing
Al Weir, Sub.
Orville Decker, Sub.
Art Hillmer, R.Wing
Allan Galbraith, L. Defense
Whit Hillmer, Centre
Bob Armstrong, Goal
John Hashek, Sub. Goal
Deke McDougall, R. Defence
Ban Taylor, Centre

A few more of the many names of those who also were outstanding in hockey over the years are: Harry Wilson, George Galbraith, Anson Lawrence, Ray Manbert, 'Bub' Macrae, Elton Grice, and Benny Marsells."

THE OAKVILLE CURLING CLUB

When the "New Rink" was built in Victoria Park in 1920 it included two curling rinks, one on each side of the middle ice surface. This was the incentive for the formation very soon afterwards of the Oakville Curling Club — another popular winter sport of the 1920s.

BADMINTON

Shortly after the First World War a surplus aeroplane hangar was bought and placed in the Oakville Fair Grounds for use as an agricultural display building. When the Oakville Fair came to an end in 1924, a Badminton Club was organized using this building, which stood on the site of the present hockey arena. It was marked out into four badminton courts, and the game caught on like wildfire, filling the gap left by the lack of tennis and golf during the winter. Badminton courts were marked out and enjoyed also in school gymnasiums and church halls. After a few years the hangar was moved and attached to the Oakville Club, where it still provides space for badminton for the members.

Badminton in the 1920s was highly competitive, both among club members and in inter-club matches. Competition from Toronto was provided by the Badminton and Racquet Club, the Carleton Club, and the teams which played in the old Armouries on University Avenue. We played with other clubs as well, in Hamilton, St. Catharines, Woodstock, and Galt. We were kept busy playing visiting matches at all these places as well as entertaining the same teams in return games on our home courts. The Oakville Club had many fine players, and was especially fortunate in having such outstanding sportswomen in both tennis and badminton as Winifred Whittington and Nora Crossley, who carried off championship after championship — Dominion, Provincial, and Inter-Club — in both doubles and singles. These two ladies made names for themselves wherever and whenever they played, not only in racquet games but also on the golf course.

SKATING

Everyone looked forward to a "good skating winter," with not too much snow to shovel to keep the outside rinks clear. Large skating areas, popular with all, were those on "the Marsh." One was slightly east of the site now occupied by the Power Boat Clubhouse, on the marshy flats between the creek and its bank below the present Fire Hall; another was on the west flats below the Tannery. Coal-oil lanterns were used for lighting, and bonfires were often kept burning for both light and warmth. A small shed was on hand for changing skates or boots. After the "New Rink" was built in 1920 in Victoria Park and skaters were not dependent upon the weather, night after night was spent there, provided the ice was not needed for hockey. Skating on Saturday nights to the Oakville Band was a highlight of the week.

ON THE SNOW

Snowshoeing, especially on a moonlit night, was fun and called for a good "feed" at someone's house afterwards. Tobogganing and sleigh-riding were keenly enjoyed down the long steep slopes of the Red Hill on the Seventh Line (Trafalgar Road) before the slope was graded, its top sliced off and replaced by town buildings and apartment houses. The Red Hill on the Eighth Line was well patronized also. Anderson's Hill at Watson and Colborne Street (Lakeshore Road) provided ample sleigh-riding and tobogganing for the younger children. Bob-sleighing was popular with many, but only safe for the more mature. There was quite an art to steering and manipulating these long sleighs on four or more fast runners and, with proper conditions and expertise, it was sometimes possible from a start at the top of the old Red Hill, at either the Seventh or the Eighth Line, to continue at high speed down over the railway tracks and beyond. Needless to say, the Queen Elizabeth Way had not yet replaced the Lower Middle Road at the time of this popular sport!

Dorothy (Chisholm) Souter remembers the fun of horse-drawn sleigh-rides, sponsored sometimes by a school or Sunday school, or privately arranged:

> "We would gather at the meeting-place decided upon, where several teams of horses stood hitched to large open sleighs, of the sort used for cartage. Straw was piled thickly on the bottom of the sleigh for warmth and generally a plank had been placed along each side to sit on — better still, on the floor! The teams stood waiting, sleigh-bells jangling, and we would pile in with our special cronies and be driven around the less-travelled roads for an hour or so, coming back to a welcome feed of cocoa and sandwiches and other refreshments."

ANOTHER "WINTER SPORT"?

While horses and cutters were trotting the snowy streets, certain children, including myself, enjoyed (unknown to our parents) what was known as "hookying-on." This entailed standing on the end of one of the back runners of a moving sleigh. (We usually enjoyed this pastime in pairs — one child to a side!) A few drivers did not take kindly to this imposition, and we knew well enough to steer clear of them; the warning flick of a whip was sometimes used as a hint to older children that they were not welcome. However, the majority were people who knew us and were very patient with our wish for a short free ride! One of our favourites was Brock Chisholm — later the famous doctor — who, with a bear-skin rug thrown over the back of his sleigh, was more often than not accompanied by his fiancée, and future wife, Grace Ryrie. The sleigh bells were always a cheery accompaniment to this "sport."

The slower-moving sleigh used for cartage resembled a low-slung, shallow, rectangular box hung over four runners and was pulled by a team of horses. We did not stand on the runners of these but sat in style on the edge of the box, ready to hop off at a moment's notice. These sleighs travelled mainly up and down "the Station Road," and were used often by the Basket Factory or Davis and Doty to carry lumber and by Ashbury's flour mill to move grain. We considered them a fine method of transportation.

SPRING AND SUMMER

A sure sign of Spring on the school grounds and wherever small boys congregated was the almost non-stop playing of marbles, alleys, or "dibs," and the beginning of "catch" and baseball. At the same time the girls were busy playing "jacks" and hopscotch, skipping, and enjoying all the outdoor games again. Once more, roller-skating enabled you to fly around town everywhere in a fraction of the walking-time, and your bicycle after its winter's rest seemed like an old friend.

When Spring and Summer arrived, the great attraction was to the many wooded areas in and near the town. Nearest at hand was "Anderson's Bush," the wooded part of the "Brantwood Survey," between Palmer and Spruce and from Douglas to Gloucester Avenue, and lovely wildflowers grew there in the thick woods. Anderson's Bush could be reached quickly after school or on weekends by children's ever-present roller-skates or bicycles. Similar lovely flowers and trees were available also by taking a slightly longer bicycle ride to any part of the Red Hill, and to numerous other woods along the nearby country roads.

In 1912, when we lived at the edge of Anderson's Bush (no.317 Gloucester), the large and graceful sweet-chestnut tree was still scattered generously through these woods and throughout southern Ontario, and we had three very large, tall ones on our property. The white "tassels" covering the trees in Spring turned, in the Fall, into delicious sweet chestnuts hidden inside prickly, green cases, and these were a delicacy that few children in the town were able to resist. Tragically, a severe blight in the 1920s and 1930s wiped out every sweet chestnut tree in the Country. Anderson's Bush had been full of them and they were greatly missed when they gradually died and had to be cut down. Later, a further great loss to the Bush was the large number of giant oaks which, although not blighted, were hacked down while healthy.

Fortunately, none of this had happened when we lived nearby and, since only two or three houses were built in the area while I was growing up, I considered these beautiful woods my own private domain! I knew each year exactly where I could be sure to find the first wildflower of all — the hepatica — which flowered before the leaf appeared. White anemones, trillium, columbine, Solomon's seal, and May-apples grew in many patches of deep shade, while the mauve wild geranium and clumps of fern and bracken seemed to be everywhere. I knew all the low swamps where marsh marigolds and the enormous, rank skunk-cabbage grew, and could be counted on to get my feet wet several times a day. Patches of wild violets — purple, yellow dog-tooth, and the small, sweet-smelling, white ones — came up in the same places each year. A few even grew sparingly in the grass along some of the sidewalks. In very deep shade, after a bit of looking, one could find the elusive "Jack-in-the-Pulpit" and the rather weird, snow-white "Indian Pipe."

Enhancing all this was the lovely sight and sound of the birds, which brought many up from downtown to watch and enjoy. My own favourite sound was that of the whippoorwill in the evening, and at night the gentle croaking of the frogs in a nearby swamp. I had good friends to share all this: I was a lucky girl. Boys found the woods a wonderful setting for "Cowboys and Indians," and girls played endless games of "House" up in the trees, under them, or in a clearing.

SUMMER ACTIVITIES

Summer meant swimming, sailing, boating, regattas, and summer-long activities on the lake and creek. Swimming — or "bathing" — was perhaps the favourite. When very small I was dressed in a bathing-suit of a most peculiar material named "lustre," which, it was said, would shed the water. Whether it did this or not, my first one, according to a photograph, boasted a large sailor-collar trimmed with white braid, and had elastic at the knees!

Summer also meant the Oakville Band. Oakville has had a band since the first Dominion Day, July 1, 1867, when it was a small military band with the 20th Halton Battalion. From 1881, when it became the Oakville Citizens' Band, it has evolved into the high calibre band of today. Between 1900 and 1930, trained under the capable leadership of Mr. W.H. Tuck and later of Mr. A.J. Locksley, the Band was in great popular demand at its well-attended, weekly concerts in the bandstands in both George's Square and Lakeside Park.

Parades of all sorts were numerous and very popular in town — and what would a parade be without the Band! It led the Sunday church parades of the "town fathers," the firemen, veterans, Masonic Lodge, Independent Order of Oddfellows, Independent Order of Foresters, and many other lodges and groups. It was indispensable also to the success of Garden Parties, and especially to the enjoyment of the annual Oakville Fair and Horse Show held in September. You may be sure that band members had very little time to themselves. The Oakville Band competed annually with others at the Canadian National Exhibition and elsewhere and won many high awards in its class. The hours and hours spent at band rehearsals, and the endless time spent in practising by the individual members, should not be overlooked or forgotten by grateful citizens.

GARDEN PARTIES AND PICNICS

Church Garden Parties were held in the evenings by each of the churches in turn during the Summer, and took place in the attractive grounds of church, manse, presbytery, or rectory. The Oakville Band made sure that the citizens were aware of the event by parading down the Main Street to the site of the Garden Party — brasses blaring, drums and big bass drum beating — and playing all the familiar pieces that were expected of it!

These events were enjoyed especially as an opportunity for friends to meet one another, and the grounds were prettily decorated with Chinese lanterns, lighting the booths set up for raising a little money. The usual attractions were there for children: races, the "fish pond" (five cents), the "orange tree," (which was a large evergreen hung with small gifts wrapped beforehand to resemble oranges), lemonade and raspberry vinegar, and, without fail, Ferrah's five-cent home-made ice-cream — in cones or otherwise.

The stage programme customarily consisted of out-of-town talent: a comic entertainer or two, a ventriloquist, and a good baritone, soprano, or tenor. During intervals between performances the Band would strike up and supply background music for the crowd. A tastefully set tableau on stage was often the finale to the evening's entertainment. Each Garden Party varied slightly from another, and all were enjoyed thoroughly.

The firemen always held a popular mammoth Garden Party in Victoria Park, often featuring the new "jitney" (ten-cent) dances in the nearby hall. The Lions' Club, other service clubs, and town organizations held large money-making Carnivals, sometimes in the Fair Grounds or on the Public School playground, known as the "common" (site of the present Centennial complex, Navy Street). These were lively affairs, featuring "crown & anchor," roulette wheels, various other games of chance, and tests of skill for prizes. Usually a car would be raffled off. The Carnivals also supplied good stage entertainment.

Many of the large estates along the lakefront opened their spacious grounds for Garden Parties or other outdoor gatherings, in aid of charitable causes such as the Canadian National Institute for the Blind, the "War Effort" (1914—18), the Red Cross, and other benefits. In early Summer, too, an outdoor Strawberry Tea, Social, or Festival, held in a garden or church, was not hard to find, and everyone enjoyed these.

The Sunday-school picnic by boat was a momentous event for the whole family, and several took place each summer. An item from an early newspaper follows:

> "At seven o'clock you could see crowds of people wending their way to the wharf, though the boat was not expected to arrive till eight. The Oakville Band was in attendance, and when the "TURBINIA" pulled out of the harbour with about 1200 Oakvillians aboard, with the sweet music and waving of handkerchiefs of those who came to see their friends off, troubles were forgotten for the day. The boat reached Toronto at about 9:30, where some went to Centre Island at once, and others went to town."

"The White Star"

This particular trip took place very early in the century, but it was followed year after year by other picnics and excursions by boat to parks on Lake Ontario, such as Grimsby, Centre Island, and Wabasso (LaSalle) Park in Burlington.

(Unfortunately, our annual Sunday-school picnic was always a bone of contention between me and my mother, who could not bring herself to allow me to join these excursions. A rare tragedy or two had been known to occur elsewhere, possibly at a pier when passengers, loading or unloading, crowded to one side of the boat causing it to capsize. To me, however, this seemed a small tragedy compared to my own in not being allowed to join the others, and my parents made up for my disappointment with other treats to take the place of the Sunday-school picnic.)

SUNNYSIDE AMUSEMENT PARK

In the 1920s the young population of town were greatly attracted to the Sunnyside Amusement Park, one of the best in the land, with its roller-coaster, Ferris wheel, dodgems, large "ten-cents-a-dance pavilion" — in fact every conceivable form of entertainment — and food. Sunnyside ran along the north side of Lakeshore Road, parallel to the wide Sunnyside beach of beautiful white sand, which reached as far as the Humber River and boasted a handsome bathing pavilion.

BOWLING GREEN and TENNIS CLUB

In 1908, at a special meeting of the town council, a lease was granted for the ground immediately south of the old Town Hall on Navy Street for use as Lawn Bowling Greens, and Mr. E. T. Lightbourn became the first president of the Lawn Bowling Club. At the same time the Tennis Club was leased ground to the rear of the Town Hall for grass tennis-courts. Although the Town Hall burned down three years later, the Lawn Bowling Club and the tennis-courts have been in constant use for over 70 years.

THE CRICKET CLUB

Early in the "teens" of the 1900s the Oakville Cricket Club was formed by a large group of enthusiastic players. Mr. Guest, headmaster of Appleby School, generously made available to them the excellent cricket pitch on the Appleby grounds while the boys were away on their summer holidays. On Saturday afternoons and holidays a crowd of spectators enjoyed good cricket amongst the Oakville members themselves, or against outside cricket elevens, such as the Toronto Cricket Club and others.

THE OAKVILLE GOLF CLUB

(with thanks for assistance to Norman Williamson and Ban Taylor)

The Oakville Golf Club was formed in the Spring of 1921 by three young men, Stuart Brown, Ban Taylor, and Frank Worrell, eager that Oakville should have a golf club of its own. Upon enquiry, they found that 55 acres of rolling fields on the Sixth Line were available, and with this knowledge, they set the wheels in motion to collect the money needed to acquire the property. They soon were lucky enough to find 100 or more influential and equally enthusiastic men who gave financial support to their venture. The property was bought; a charter was secured by the aforementioned Mr. Brown, a lawyer; and Mr. E.T. Lightbourn was elected first president of the Oakville Golf Club. The course was laid out by a man of much experience, Mr. George Cummings, pro at the Toronto Golf Club, and his young son, Lou, was the first pro of the newly formed club.

Because of their keenness for tennis as well as golf, Stuart Brown and Ban Taylor saw to it that a fine tennis-court was laid out. This was near the old clubhouse, in the approximate vicinity of the present parking-lot. The court was a boon to the minority of us who, although we played golf too, still preferred tennis. As an added attraction for us, this court was available for use on Sundays, when play was not permitted at the Oakville Club in the centre of town.

At the time the Oakville Golf Club opened in 1921 the trip up or down the Sixth Line was an easy matter. (This was, of course, before the Lower Middle Road and the old "High Level Bridge" over the river were replaced by the Queen Elizabeth Way.) On leaving Dundas Street at the Sixth Line (Old Mill Road) we simply followed the creek bank — Ashbury home on the left at the curve; Glassco's Jam Factory on the right — and continued over the level crossing at the C.N.R. tracks. The Sixth Line followed the creek bank close to the edge, giving a lovely view through the trees to the river far below and to the old mill dam, which was a favourite swimming-hole for the boys, skinny-dipping, in Summer. Passing on the left the pretty shaded Town Cemetery with picket fence, we crossed the Lower Middle Road and, in a matter of minutes, turned in at the entrance to the Oakville Golf Club.

Because of the somewhat diagonal northwest course of the Sixth Line along the river bank, this was a slightly shorter route than the alternative one of continuing up Dundas Street to the Lower Middle Road, turning left to the Sixth Line, and then proceeding right for the short distance to the Golf Club. Either route was simple and direct.

BASEBALL

From the early 1900s baseball enjoyed great popularity in Oakville. A newspaper account of one event in 1904 follows:

> "About 200 people turned out to watch the Baseball Match which was played last Tuesday between the merchants of the north and south sides of Colborne Street. Constable Felan was the umpire."

D. Chapman, owner of the Basket Factory, had a keen interest in and was manager of the Oakville baseball teams. His son Robert recalls the local enthusiasm for the game:

> "After the Oakville Fair moved across the creek to its larger grounds on Rebecca Street, the old Fair Grounds were renamed Victoria Park and were then used during the entire season for baseball, lacrosse, and

football team practice. Among some early basebell players were Wally Wales, Arthur Felan, Johnnie Williams, and the two Tizard brothers, Art and Fred.

"The game fell off, understandably, during the First World War, when many of the team were overseas. However, by the 1920s it was taken up again with renewed enthusiasm. The following baseball team, with D. Chapman as manager, won the Halton County league in 1922:
Whit Hillmer — Pitcher and First Base
Don Davis — Pitcher
Allan Galbraith — Catcher
Anson Lawrence — Centre Field
Art Tizard — Infield
Art Hillmer — Right Field
E. Southwick — Outfielder
Hiram Williams — Pitcher and Outfield
Deke McDougall — Infield
George Galbraith — Infield
Ollie Johnson — Shortstop
George Snowball — Left Field
Benny Languay — Centre Field
Cecil Harker — Right Field
Freddie Green — Third Base
Elton Grice — Second Base

Some other notable players of those years were: George Fletcher, Maurice Felan, Darby Hall, Harvey Lyons, Norm Carter, Cliff Post, Jack Markey, and Harry and Doug Wilson.

"Oakville's tremendous enthusiasm for its baseball teams prompted Mr. J. M. Wallace, once owner of the Oakville Basket Factory, generously to provide flood-lighting for the baseball diamond in Victoria Park, which, thereafter, was re-named Wallace Park. A grandstand — or bleachers — was erected facing the diamond on the Allan Street side of the park. The flood-lights were transferred several years ago to the Bronte Ball Park and are still in use there."

THE AGGIE: YACHT OF DISTINCTION

The *Aggie* was the most famous product of Oakville's shipyards, and Hazel C. Mathews recalled :

"Captain James Andrew (1846-1918), first a sailor on the Great

The "Aggie"

Lakes, next engaged in shipbuilding, travelling across Canada to build schooners on many waters. Captain Andrew soon gained a reputation for fast sailing-ships, and about 1861 he established a shipyard at the foot of William Street, below the bridge which crossed The Sixteen on Colborne Street (Lakeshore Road).

"But eventually steamers replaced the schooners as carriers, and it was then that Captain Andrew turned to building the pleasure-yachts for which he was to become famous. His first yacht, the *Aggie*, was commissioned by the owners of the Tannery, Cecil G. Marlatt and Christoper Armstrong. This yacht, named in honour of Mr. Marlatt's first wife, was destined to bring Captain Andrew great renown as a builder of fast ships. To quote from the *"Annals of the Royal Canadian Yacht Club"*, The '*Aggie* was to become the most successful yacht under the R.C.Y.C. burgee, accumulating no fewer than 83 winning flags in the course of a long career.'

"In the early 1900s the *Aggie*'s skipper, Cecil G. Marlatt, was Commodore, Vice-Commodore, and Rear-Commodore of the R.C.-Y.C., flying his flag from the *Aggie*'s rigging. If unable to race the *Aggie* himself, the Commodore sent her to Toronto on a Friday so that she might be ready to be raced on the week-end by another skipper and crew from the Yacht Club. She won the majority of races for the Club.

"The skipper often took a number of his daughter's young friends sailing of an afternoon, when they were permitted to sit along the 'down' side of the yacht and trail their feet. However, they quickly learned to lie flat when the order was given to 'come about.' Any who were slow to obey were not invited again. When aboard the yacht, one chose a place and remained in it!

"Upon the failure of the Tannery the yacht was sold and, when driven ashore in a gale, was wrecked not far from the farm which had provided her timbers. The *Aggie* was 57 years of age. During the Second World War when the Corvette H.M.C.S. *Oakville* was commissioned at the mouth of The Sixteen and sailed away into the Atlantic on convoy duty, she carried aboard the ship's clock of the *Aggie*."

THE YACHT *CANADA*

The yacht *Canada*, which was originally responsible for the annual Canada's Cup Match,[8] famous throughout the 1900s, was also built in the Oakville shipyards of Captain James Andrew. It is included here since sailing, competitive and otherwise, was of such prime importance in the port of Oakville both before and after the turn of the century. There were very close ties with the Royal Canadian Yacht Club and, after the opening of the Oakville Club in 1908, yacht races between the two clubs became a part of the life of the town.

The following is an account of the origin of the yacht *Canada*, extracted from "The Autobiography of Æmilius Jarvis" and contributed by his daughter, Augusta.

"In the winter of 1895-1896 the Lincoln Park Yacht Club of Chicago challenged the Royal Canadian Yacht Club of Toronto to a series of races between a yacht they were building called the Vincedor [VENCEDOR], and a comparable yacht to be built by the R.C.Y.C. to meet this challenge. A syndicate was formed by the R.C.Y.C., and Rear Commodore Æmilius Jarvis was appointed Skipper of the proposed yacht, to be built to meet the American Challenger's specifications.

"The CANADA was designed by William Fyfe of Scotland and her frame and pattern for the keel were shipped to Oakville where, in April of 1896, Captain James Andrew was commissioned to build her. This he accomplished in record speed and in July, 1896, the yacht was named CANADA and christened by the eight-year-old daughter of Æmilius Jarvis, Mary Powell Jarvis. The CANADA sailed her first race on July 27th, 1896. . . .

The "Canada's" Cup

"Her first 'BEST OUT OF THREE' Race with her prime competitor, the VINCEDOR took place near Toledo at the west end of Lake Erie. The first race of the three, due to lack of wind, was called off — the CANADA being in the lead at the time.

"The Second Race on the same course next day resulted in a finish by the CANADA of a lead of twenty-three minutes.

"The following day, the two yachts raced in winds 20—25 m.p.h. — with occasional squalls. Each yacht took turns several times of being in the lead, with the CANADA ultimately winning by *twenty-six seconds*!

"The Cup presented by the City of Toledo was made by Tiffany's of New York — a very handsome silver bowl, supported by a crouching Lion on one side and an Eagle on the other.

"On returning to Toronto a wonderful reception was given the CANADA and Crew. All the steamers and yachts turned out and 'dressed ship', and the Crew was honoured by the City of Toronto."

Rear-Commodore Æmilius Jarvis and his partners joined in presenting this first cup, won by the *Canada*, to the Royal Canadian

Yacht Club in Toronto, as trustees, "to be held for International Racing between yachts representing Yacht Clubs on the Great Lakes, either in Canada or the United States, and to be known as "CANADA'S CUP." Captain Andrew built several more contenders and challengers for the Canada's Cup, some of them skippered by Æmilius Jarvis, before Andrew's shipyard was sold in 1915.

Miss Augusta Jarvis, to whom I am indebted for the interesting information concerning her late father, Æmilius Jarvis, and the Canada's Cup, has, in addition, supplied information relating to a further important tie with Oakville. Upon being selected to skipper the new yacht, Æmilius Jarvis loaded his wife, family, and some pieces of furniture, including a baby's crib, on to a barge and brought them from Toronto to Oakville. He did this with the dual purpose of establishing the family in a summer cottage on the lakefront west and of overseeing Captain Andrew's building of the *Canada*, which was then in full swing.

Perhaps because of a rough trip on Lake Ontario Mrs. Jarvis, quite soon after her arrival in Oakville, proceeded to give birth to her daughter, Augusta. This happy event occurred with the professional attendance of Dr. John Urquhart, whose importance in the town is referred to earlier, with the assistance of Mrs. Urquhart, during the very early hours of a summer morning!

Owing to her father's preoccupation with the *Canada* in the nearby shipyard, however, he quite forgot to register Augusta's birth, and it was not until after his death in 1940 that this fact was discovered! Augusta was christened in St. Jude's Church and it was found later that the Rector had confused surname and Christian name, with the result that the child appeared on the Church records as Augusta Æmillius, instead of Augusta Jarvis.

THE OAKVILLE FAIR AND HORSE SHOW

The Oakville Fair and Horse Show in early September gave a hint of the end of summertime. It had evolved from the Agricultural Fair, organized in 1880 and held in Trafalgar Square when the Agricultural Hall (site of the present Curling Club) was built there for showing and judging produce, livestock, flowers, handcrafts, and home-baking. Artwork and handwriting done by the pupils of the Public School were keenly contested at the Fair and great pains were taken to have one's work awarded a First, Second, or Third Ribbon. In the early 1900s a special feature was the parade on Opening Day of all the Public School children, led by the Oakville Band and marching to the Fair, each child waving a small Union Jack.

The old Fair Grounds, between Allan and Reynolds streets, soon proved inadequate and in 1913 assumed the name Victoria Park (now Wallace Park). The town then acquired a new and larger Fair Grounds of ten or more acres on Rebecca Street at the head of Brant Street; this property was named Trafalgar Park. The new Fair Grounds in Trafalgar Park included, through the efforts of Hughie Wilson, H.C. Cox, and others, a large grandstand overlooking the show-ring. Stables, stock buildings, a "mini-midway," and other show buildings were added. These allowed for considerable expansion of the Fair and led to its incorporation with the Horse Show, for which Oakville became famous far and wide. It was then known officially as the "Oakville Fair and Horse Show," lasting three days in mid-September. Highly competitive contests in jumping and general horsemanship took place both between local stables and with visiting ones.

The Oakville Fair and Horse Show

The presence at the Fair of the Ennisclare Hunt Club attracted other hunt clubs, and this was a sight to behold, with the riders all in their "pink" and the many hunters, jumpers, and hounds. Among famous competitive stables were, east of the town, those of Harry Giddings, many times a winner of the King's Plate, and Ryland New, who later won the King's Plate with "Troutlet." The stables of Walter Harland Smith, on the east side of the Seventh Line above the Upper Middle Road, had a high reputation. His daughter, Carol (Smith) Cox,[9] was an expert horsewoman and carried off ribbon after ribbon in competitions here and elsewhere. Mr. Harland Smith's spanking turn-out of coach and four-in-hand was always looked forward to in front of the grandstand, at the Fair and at many other events. Hughie Wilson won numerous prizes at the Fair, and far and wide, with thoroughbreds trained in his stables and arena at the northwest corner of the Seventh Line and the Lower Middle Road as well as with those trained at the Ennisclare Stables. Many others with their private mounts competed also in jumping and showing at the annual Horse Show.

In addition to the Horse Show, elaborate Extravaganzas and Pageants, involving casts of 100 or more, were staged in front of the grandstand year after year. The exceptionally talented Norma (Smith) Gairdner[6] was the leading light in the production of most of these events and was assisted, among others, by an outstanding "showman," Mr. W. Ward-Price,[10] then a resident of Oakville. The grandstand shows were enhanced by Mr. Ward-Price who acted as ringmaster, made all announcements, and generally directed ceremonies during the performances. Unfortunately, after providing many years of enjoyment, the Oakville Fair and Horse Show came to an end in 1924.

OLD HOME WEEK

In 1924, as a result of tireless planning and organization, Oakville's "Old Boys and Girls" from both near and far were invited to join together in August for four days of festivities and renewing old acquaintances. Families in town generously provided accommodation for all those returning to visit their old Home Town. On registering, each was identified with his or her name framed in a sturdy brooch of simulated copper, matching a large commemorative copper coin, which was suspended from the brooch and engraved on one side with the Oakville Lighthouse and on the reverse with the words, "Oakville Old Boys & Girls Reunion, Aug. 2, 3, 4 & 5, 1924." Each was given also "Oakville's Welcome Key," a symbol "Entitling Old Boys and Girls to the Freedom of Oakville."

Old Home Week was an important event at that time, and is permanently recorded by two panoramic photographs in the possession of the Oakville Historical Society. One shows many hundreds attending a gathering, which we would now call an "Ecumenical" Service, in front of the large grandstand on the Fair Grounds, with the full Oakville Citizens' Band on hand for hymn-singing. The other presents the full complement of "Old Boys and Girls" and town officials attending the closing banquet and ceremonies of the reunion. Church Street between Thomas and George streets had been closed off, and the banquet tables set up in the street. The photographer had stood at the site of the present Post Office, the "new" Fire Hall (1922) and the Masonic Hall (1923) on his right, to catch this priceless photographic record of Oakville's "Old Boys and Girls, 1924."

Footnotes:

[1] A few of these included: Enrico Caruso, Madame Galli-Curci, Percy Grainger, Jascha Heifetz, Madame Schumann Heink, Fritz Kreisler, Harry Lauder, Lily Pons, Sergei Rachmaninov, Lawrence Tibbett, and the dancer Nazimova, as well as perennial performances of the Toronto, Philadelphia, New York, and other symphony orchestras and the Toronto Mendelssohn Choir.
[2] Among these were: "The Merry Widow," "The Pink Lady," "Chu Chin Chow," "The Maid of the Mountains," Gilbert and Sullivan operettas performed by the D'Oyly Carte Company of England, and such Sigmund Romberg operettas as "Maytime," "The Student Prince," "The Desert Song," "Blossom Time," and "The New Moon."
[3] The Princess Theatre, equal in popularity with the Royal Alexandra, stood on the south side of King Street in Toronto. The extension of University Avenue south of King Street resulted in the demolition of the Princess Theatre and other buildings on the same street.
[4] The Grand Theatre stood until the early 1920s on the south side of Adelaide Street West in Toronto. The fate of its owner, Ambrose J. Small, last seen in his theatre late one evening, has remained a mystery to this day.
[5] Gregory Theatre: see p. 99.
[6] Norma Gairdner: daughter of Walter Harland Smith; wife of James A. Gairdner.
[7] Known to her many nieces and nephews and to other Chisholm relatives as "Auntie Kate."

[8] From the *Globe and Mail*, Sept. 12, 1981:

> "The Canada's Cup has been the symbol of match-racing supremacy on the Great Lakes since 1896 when Æmelius Jarvis of the Royal Canadian Yacht Club beat a yacht called Vencedor from the Lincoln Park Club of Chicago 2-0 in the best-of-three series. Jarvis named the cup after his winning yacht, Canada, and put it up as a perpetual trophy. . .
>
> "To-morrow [Sept. 13] will be the 15th meeting of what has become the oldest continuing sporting event held between the two nations."

The victory was Canada's this year; won by *COUG* of the Royal Hamilton Yacht Club over *BLACK MAJIC* of Detroit's Bayview Yacht Club.

[9] Carol (Smith) Cox: wife of Wilfrid M. Cox.

[10] W. Ward-Price: see p. 95.

Lawn Bowling Club, 1916

Front Row (L to R): Rev. W.B. Smith, Charles Green, Louis Coté, A.G. Biette, L. Kemp.

Back Row (L to R): Hubert Chisholm, ?, Prof. G.A. Guess, W. Walsh, J. Strachan, Christopher Armstrong, T.G. Ruddell, L.H. Bedlington, Vavasor Robin.

12
An Era of Gracious Living

At Hazel Mathews' request, Mary (Marlatt) Oliver wrote the following recollections of her years from 1900 to 1930.

"My father, Cecil Marlatt, built the family house (no.43 Dunn Street) for his bride in 1888. Their son, Kenneth, was born there and his mother died a few years later. Father then married my mother and they had three daughters, Marjorie, Betty, and myself (Mary). To the family should be added members of the household: Minnie McCulloch, our faithful housekeeper, lived with us from our childhood days, as did Martha Adams, our beloved cook, who contributed much cheerfully given comfort to us all. Martha was a tribute to her own cooking and it need only be said that she wore a size 54 comfortably! Martha's grandparents, slaves from the southern United States, arrived in Canada by the historic "Underground Railway," and their children, one of whom was Martha's father, were born, and were highly respected citizens of Bronte all their lives.

"Our house faced Dunn Street at the southwest corner of the six-lot block bounded by Dunn, King, Dundas, and William streets. Mr. Robert Barclay's house and garden occupied the lot at the northwest corner of this block. Towards the lake, across King Street (no.31 Dunn), lived our special and dear friends, the Lightbourn family. Many years of happiness were spent with Harvey, Audrey, Lesley, and Ruth. The garden along William, Dundas, and part way along King was surrounded by a high, white board-fence, while a lower picket-fence ran parallel with our house on King Street and as far as the Barclay property on Dunn Street. In front of the house were gates for each of the two

Home of C.G. Marlatt (northeast corner Dun and King Streets)

curved sidewalks leading to the front verandah. These gates had always to be removed before Hallowe'en night and put in the cellar, or they would disappear up in trees, suffering in company with anything movable and with outdoor 'toilets,' which were pretty sure to be overturned during the 'innocent' celebration of Hallowe'en.

"Flower beds, about two feet wide, were planted mostly with salvia and cannas around the garden along the fence. Several varieties of apple trees grew on the King Street side of the garden, while on the north side were English cherry trees — red and black. Here also were two cement 'pools.' One of these was about two or three feet deep and we could swim in it when we were little; in the smaller pool were water-lilies and goldfish. In that part of the garden was the root cellar, covered over with grass, where vegetables were stored during the winter. A 'pagoda' stood nearby and also a small, separated part with what we called our 'mud-pie house,' which was used later to attempt to raise pheasants, and to keep rabbits. A greenhouse and small tool-house stood near Mr. Barclay's fence and a few fir-trees flanked a walk leading to the back entrance of the house. Vegetables were grown on our property on the south side of King Street near the barn, where Betty's pony and the other horses were stabled, as well as 'Jersey,' our cow. A garage was later built in place of the barn.

"On that property was our tennis-court and also space for cricket games and croquet. Two summer-houses, with seats around three of the sides, were placed so that one could either look at the lake or watch tennis or other games. Afternoon tea was brought from the house if there was a tennis party, cricket game, or even croquet. There are photographs showing the girls with 'hats' on for tennis: tiny waists and long skirts, often with the addition of a short train!

Girl dressed for tennis, early 1900s

"As children our job was to pick the blackberries and for this activity we wore black cotton stockings and full gym bloomers. We felt the bushes had real arms which stretched out and scratched our legs regardless of the stockings. We picked the delicious 'Golden Bantam' corn and cut asparagus, which were both cooked immediately to retain the mouth-watering flavour. We gathered a very few eggs from our little hen-house each day, and Father contended that the eggs cost him $1.00 each! We raised a few pigeons, and so occasionally had squab for a special dinner — a whole one each, beautifully cooked by Black Martha. (Martha's favourite dish was calves' liver, which she called 'velvet steak.')

"Enormous mushrooms grew in our cellar in a dark spot near the furnace. Our wine cellar was there also, and a large cupboard with holes in the doors for ventilation, which held jams and fruit preserves. This cupboard also held a large crock of home-made mincemeat, which Martha began mixing in October each year, using plenty of brandy, to be ready at Christmas-time. Made about the same time, and kept in the cool cellar, were tin moulds of plum puddings. These have been known to keep perfectly for a year. Martha's bathroom was in the cellar also, containing a huge, old, tin (or metal) bathtub with gold lions' feet and a board-trim around the top.

"The old kitchen had a wooden floor, which Martha got down on her knees to scrub with a large, hand scrub-brush and a soapy mixture of old fats and lime. The latter were all melted together, put in a large crock, and kept in the wash-room, which opened off the kitchen. The kitchen was a large one and it took poor Martha some time to cover the ground. The adjoining room held also our old ice refrigerator and a bench on which stood two wash-tubs, to one of which was attached a wringer, which had to be turned by hand to squeeze out the water after rinsing. The flat pieces were put through a heated mangle. Used frequently here was a small iron affair which, when heated, restored frills and pleats on blouses and other clothing when they were passed through it. Another iron instrument here was one on which was placed a piece of steak. A top was screwed down and this extracted the beef juice, or beef tea. When ill, we were given a little of this to drink, with thin fingers of home-made bread.

"Another 'member of the family,' 'Polly', our parrot, gave us much pleasure. She used to call the gardener 'John'[1] and Martha 'Black Cook' — to which Martha always replied, 'As long as you don't call me "Bad Cook"!' When we covered up her cage at night, she always said in a soft voice 'Good Night.' We hung her cage from a large ceiling-hook on the verandah at times and, one day, had to rush to get it down when Oakville had one of its very rare tornadoes. This one blew Mrs. Hugh Calverley over a fence on their Seventh Line (Trafalgar Road) farm and blew down a huge, old elm tree in our garden, demolishing one brick chimney and destroying what Kenneth's little son called the 'tin embroidery' along the top of our front verandah. This was judged 'an act of God' — and so no insurance!

"The mantel-top in the front parlour held Royal Doulton china figures — two lovely figurines: a lady with an open fan, and a gentleman bowing gracefully, facing each other — and, between them, a pretty glass-enclosed ormolu clock. On either side of the fireplace stood several iron pieces made in Japan, including a large fish, a jar for rose-petals, and a Buddah. These had been brought home by Captain Francis J. Brown (no.289 Trafalgar) from voyages to Japan, and given to his wife in Oakville, who had a small store and sold these articles to Oakvillites for an income. There was a pretty Persian rug in the room and a much-used Heintzman piano. (An unwritten law: 'nothing but hymns allowed on Sundays.') Among some favourite pictures were two 'London Cries' painted by E. Wheatley, R.A. (plates 4 and 7 from a set of 12,) and two Baxter prints, 'Warwick Lady Chapel' and 'Queen Caroline's Meeting with Jennie Deans.' Baxter's colour 'mixture' was never discovered, and was very fine.

"Heavy double velour curtains hung on the parlour windows and the doorways into the library and the hall. These two doorways had sliding doors, which disappeared into the walls when not required for privacy. We had afternoon tea in the drawing-room if we had guests — and in the library, if alone. For tea, tasty watercress sandwiches might be served, or cucumber, and sometimes parsley or asparagus sandwiches (nicely rolled). Usually there was a large 'Martha' cake, either with fluffy, white boiled-icing and freshly grated coconut or with thick chocolate icing, but sometimes the cake was a pound cake topped with peel, etc.

"Those were calling-card days, with the inevitable silver card-tray on the hall table, ready to receive the calling-cards of those who arrived for tea, or otherwise. An agreed-upon day of the month was customarily set aside when a hostess was known to be 'at home' — a different day for each hostess. Thus, let us say, 'the second Tuesday' of the month might be 'Mrs. Marlatt's' day, when many callers came to meet their friends and to have a pleasant tea-hour. Afternoon Bridge parties were popular with my mother and her friends. Occasionally, there were family prayers, when the coachman, gardener, and maids would join the family in the library — particularly when we had visitors!

"On 'important occasions,' such as Marjorie's 'coming-out party,'[2] Coles, the famous caterers from Toronto, would take charge and bring their own maids and their delicious 'goodies.' Everyone of that era remembers Michie's celebrated grocery store in Toronto. Father would often stop there to carry home some of their delicious specialties: bacon, sausages, coffee, tea, and sometimes little biscuits shaped like almonds and other nuts, with a mouth-watering filling of chocolate or cream.

"Our dining-room table was mahogany with five or six extra leaves and an asbestos cover to go under the large linen cloth. Matching the table were the sideboard and buffet, and over the fireplace was a small liquor cabinet. On the mantel-shelf stood large shells, which we delighted to hold to our ears and hear the ocean roar!

"Martha made two deep berry pies each Summer, favourites of Father's: one black currant, the other gooseberry. We ate them under pressure and only if allowed plenty of 'Jersey's' thick cream, deluged with sugar and with a grate of nutmeg. Pancakes were a treat, made by Martha on a big iron griddle, which covered the *two* top stove-holes (coal, then). These floated in real maple syrup and butter, as Martha carried in more and more from the kitchen — piled high, and piping hot! Charlotte russe, flavoured with sherry, maple mousse, and 'floating island' custard might be served when visitors were present and, last but not least, Martha's strawberry shortcake. A huge round tea-biscuit (not cake) was split when hot and buttered at once. Both halves were then spread thickly with mashed and sugared strawberries, and the whole piled high with whipped cream. Father, who was on a strict diet, insisted that since his diet allowed him *fruit*, it was quite permissible for him to eat this dessert!

"Mother liked to make bread and would mix it the night before and put it beside a radiator all night to rise, covered with blankets. She kept out a little of the dough to make sweet vanilla rolls, which were lovely — as was the bread. At Father's 'Whist Club,' which included Mr. Lightbourn, Mr. Davis, Mr. Cavers, Mr. Armstrong, and others (I think eight men), they always liked to have whiskey with onion sandwiches, and to smoke cigars. So, when we were put to bed, the bedroom transoms were tightly closed, and the heavy downstairs curtains smelled of cigar smoke for a few days afterwards. Somewhat the same fare, although more substantial, was the custom on our yacht, the *Aggie*, on week-ends at Port Dalhousie and elsewhere: onion sandwiches on Ferrah's good bread; thick steaks from McDonald's, the butcher (not 'Big Mac'!); fried potatoes; afterwards coffee and fruit. An important part of our life in Summer was our yacht the *Aggie*, which is described in another chapter.[3]

"There were seven bedrooms in our house (three of them in the attic). Marjorie and I shared one, which had a fireplace. Dr. Teskey took out my appendix in that room — an acute case — since an ambulance to Toronto was unheard of in those days. A wide 'board' was borrowed from Mr. Buckle, the butcher, who had fortunately had one made a short time before, for his own operation! Convalescing, I was allowed to have a cannel-coal fire in the little bedroom fireplace, and loved watching the shadows on the wall at night.

"We could sleep in our spare room as a 'treat' at times and loved the big old brass bed, with curtains the same as the window chintz. A commode-stand was by the bed and a marble basin with hot and cold running water stood on a square of white marble. A large chintz-covered couch, with a top one could lift to discover surprising articles, possibly purchased, and forgotten, from Murray-Kay's or Eaton's stores in Toronto. One might even discover a hidden Christmas present or two — but very seldom! The large wardrobe in Mother's bedroom was mahogany and, by some means, it had come from Jamaica after an earthquake there. We used to say it would make four coffins! Mother always had her breakfast brought to her in bed.

"Up in the attic the playroom — in the tower — was also used as Kenneth's bedroom, when he was not in Toronto as a boarder at Upper Canada College. Another bedroom housed our housekeeper, Minnie, and Betty, and there were two maids' bedrooms. The tower in the playroom had three deep windows with iron bars and, at play one day, our dear friend Ruth Lightbourn managed to get just her head through the bars, and could be heard outside, distinctly and understandably, from quite a distance away. Minnie, somewhat to the discomfort of Ruth's ears, managed to pull her back to safety! Also in the attic was a ladder leading to a platform on which were two pails filled with water, and a push-up door in the roof — in case of fire. Kenneth told us that a "bogyman" lived up there, and we and the Lightbourns were terrified at the thought. A rather clever way for Kenneth to get rid of us!

"Thinking of the playroom brings back memories of the dear French dolls — long since departed — with their lovely pink-satin dresses and eyes that closed. One wound a key in their backs and, if you held the doll by the hand, she would walk across the room with you. These dolls, among other treasures, arrived in crates from France after some of Father's business trips there. On arrival the crates were brought into the library, and opened to reveal such delights as the dolls, French china, hats, etc. We each had a 'leghorn' hat, trimmed with daisies and with brown velvet ribbon that hung half-way down our backs. These were worn first of all to church on Easter Sunday, as were a pair of French white-kid gloves. I loved the smell of these and was scolded for smelling them during the sermon! We usually wore a new suit (home-made by Minnie) for Easter, and admired our new patent-leather slippers. Incidentally, 'no questions asked' — church at 11:00 a.m.; Sunday school at 2:00 p.m.; and, when we were older, church again at 7:00 p.m.

"Mother organized the concerts in our church, Knox Presbyterian, to raise money for the Ladies' Aid. When the church acquired the lovely new Cassavant organ, and the chancel had been built, she used to get good performers for piano and organ duets, such as Reginald Stewart and Reginald Godden, and Healey Willan and Viggo Kiehl, as well as sopranos and violinists. The young people were expected to go from house to house beforehand selling tickets for these performances, and everyone raced to be first at Becky Wass's, Colborne Street and Centre Avenue, as she could always be counted on to buy four. On these occasions we usually had three to dinner, and these guests stayed overnight and had breakfast with us. Once the well-known soloist Sara Barkin was one of three guests. Mother had provided a gorgeous roast of beef (with undercut!), but it turned out that Sara couldn't eat the beef, being an orthodox Jewess, and Mother felt so badly, though she certainly could not be blamed. (In those days, there was no frozen food to call on!)

"At Mother's first concert, before the chancel was built and when the inadequate old organ was still in place, she got Ernest MacMillan (later Sir Ernest) to come and perform for $25. This was during the First World War and he had just returned from a German prison camp. In later years, I don't think $25 would have been quite sufficient for a performance by Sir Ernest. Earlier than that, she did have one performer, an Englishman, who recited "Enoch Arden" to an extremely poor piano accompaniment — a deadly evening. Afterwards, coming out of the church, some man spoke to Mother and said: 'Mrs. Marlatt, in all sincerity, I think we should all be given our money back.' (This would have been the large sum of 25 cents.)

"The first movie I ever saw in Oakville was in the Town Hall on Navy Street, over the old Lock-up, north of the lovely 'Erchless.' About eight of us went in a group to see this original French Pathé film, which moved so fast we could barely follow it, much less understand it. I'm afraid we all got hysterical and behaved very badly. After the Town Hall burned down, the movies became very popular at Victoria Hall, with its floor covered with sawdust and rows of wooden kitchen chairs. Admission was about 10 cents and someone played the piano on the platform during the entire performance. One movie, attended by my sister Betty and myself, dutifully escorted by Martha, is clearly remembered because Betty refused to go home until we had seen it twice through. The movie was 'Dante's Inferno' and her enthusiasm resulted in Betty's having nightmares all that night.

"We witnessed an hilarious 'live' production of the play 'Uncle Tom's Cabin,' put on by a visiting troupe of players at Victoria Hall (admission 10 cents). The wire that carried 'Little Eva' up to heaven would not work, and she ascended in jerks, receiving no sympathy whatever from the riotous audience! The two poor old hounds in the play had to be literally shoved over the imitation ice. One hound had pups the next day — at the Oakville Hotel. My father-in-law bought one of these for 25 cents and named him 'Czar'; he grew to be enormous and was "one of the family" for many years.

"Those were busy and very happy years."

Group at "Mount Vernon"

Because of the absence of any of the labour-saving devices we have today, housekeeping in 1900-30 was "work" with a capital "W," and a good deal of extra help was needed, not so much to allow the lady of the house to enjoy a free and easy time, but because, without considerable help, the performance of the heavy household tasks would have been a physical impossibility for a single pair of hands. Good household help, luckily, was readily available to most homes before the First World War, and Oakvillites thus enjoyed the freedom to lead busy social lives. As mentioned in the chapter "Recreation, 1900-1930," the town boasted an unusually large number of spacious houses and many prosperous residents, and the stage was therefore set for a most pleasurable state of entertainment and enjoyment. The custom of paying and receiving afternoon calls among friends occupied several days in a week, and large tea and card parties (first Whist, then Bridge and Euchre) were frequently enjoyed, as were both formal and informal evening affairs.

This way of life was, to a greater or lesser degree, pretty much the rule after the turn of the century — a leftover, no doubt, from the "gay nineties" and previous years — and was only brought to an end with the First World War years. This is not to say that a round of gaiety did not exist from the war years to the 1930s, but the same quality of "style," or grandeur if you like, never quite returned after "The Great War."

Footnotes

[1] John Parnaby made himself generally indispensable in driving and looking after the horses and garden. Later, Father had him taught the mysteries of the automobile, and he became our invaluable chauffeur as well.

[2] It was the custom in this era, 1900-30, for parents to launch their daughters into society by means of a "coming-out dance," after which the daughter became a debutante. Her debut was a strictly formal, ballroom affair and often took place in the Crystal Ballroom of the King Edward Hotel in Toronto, where the music was supplied for many years by Luigi Romanelli and his orchestra. A large "coming-out" afternoon tea, or a tea-dance, was popular also as a means of highlighting what was considered to be an important milestone in a girl's life.

[3] For details of the *Aggie* see p. 172-4.

[4] Sir Ernest MacMillan: renowned conductor of the Toronto Symphony Orchestra and the Toronto Mendelssohn Choir.

Appendix

ORIGIN OF STREET NAMES

OAKVILLE STREETS SHOWN ON ORIGINAL MAP OF 1830s

(*Named by William Chisholm*: some for their locations or importance; others for his friends, members of his family, business connections, and influential men of the day who helped, in their own way, in the founding of Oakville)

ALLAN

The Hon. William Allan: first postmaster and customs collector for York (Toronto); first president of the Bank of Upper Canada; important business connection of William Chisholm.

ANDERSON (Bath Street)

Thomas Brown Anderson: head of the Montreal branch of Forsyth, Richardson and Company.*

BOND & HEAD

Sir Francis Bond Head: lieutenant governor of Upper Canada, 1836-37, following Sir John Colborne.

BRANT

Joseph Brant: chief of the Six Nations; a friend of William Chisholm.

BROCK

James Brock: a relative of General Sir Isaac Brock of War of 1812 fame.

*The firm of Forsyth, Richardson & Company, with which William Chisholm had direct business dealings, was prominent in the general trading and forwarding business, banking, canal building, and other interests.

BURNET

David Burnet: merchant of Quebec City, in the forwarding and distributing business.

CHISHOLM

Named for obvious reasons

CHURCH

Church Street originally ran through to the creek bank west of Navy Street. At this location stood the first village meeting-hall, used for a school on week-days and on Sundays for *Church* services. This has been the only explanation ever put forward for the name of this street.

COLBORNE

Sir John Colborne: a leading general commanding a regiment at the Battle of Waterloo. Shortly after Oakville was founded, as lieutenant governor of Upper Canada, he was instrumental in improving the Lakeshore route; hence the street name honouring him.

DIVISION (MacDonald Road)

Division Street formed the original northern boundary of the village of Oakville, "with the wilderness beyond." It later became the southern limit of the farm of John A. Chisholm, second son of William Chisholm and grandfather of Hazel.

DUNDAS (Trafalgar Road)

It is thought that this Oakville street, so vital to the village's communication with the outside world, was so named as an indication that it led up to the all-important "Dundas Street" (Highway no.5), running from York (Toronto) to Dundas, Hamilton, and points west. *Henry Dundas* was secretary of state for the colonies.

DUNN

The Hon. John Henry Dunn: receiver general of Upper Canada, 1820s; president of the board of directors of the Welland Canal, of which William Chisholm was a member.

FORSYTH

James Bell Forsyth: a partner in the firm of Forsyth, Richardson & Company.*

* See * p. 191.

FRONT

When the only approach to Upper Canada was by water, townships were laid out along the St. Lawrence, Lake Ontario, and the Niagara River. The shoreline was the *front* of a township, and the village of that period was laid out from this point by the surveyor.

GEORGE
JOHN

Members of the Chisholm family.

KERR

Robert W. Kerr: deputy provincial surveyor, who drew up the official map of Oakville.

KING

George King: who married Barbara, William Chisholm's sister, died during the war of 1812. His son, William McKenzie King, built "King's Castle", Sixth Line.

NAVY

Named for the great pride and enthusiasm felt by all residents for the British Navy in the wars of the early 1800s.

PALMER

Edward Palmer: a barrister, who drew the Plan of Oakville, 1835.

RANDALL

Jacob Randall, worked with William Chisolm in establishing the Oakville Harbour. He became owner of his own shipyard, was allotted Lot 1 in the original Plan of Oakville, and lived on the street which bears his name. He was tragically drowned in the wreck of one of his own ships on the lake at a comparatively early age (see p. 151).

REBECCA

Rebecca Silverthorn: the wife of William Chisholm

REYNOLDS

Charles Reynolds, whose home, it is said, was the present no.220 Reynolds Streeet, and his store on the southwest corner of Colborne Street (Lakeshore Road) and Reynolds Street.

ROBINSON

Believed to be named after *Chief Justice Sir John Beverly Robinson*, Toronto.

SHEDDON

Thomas Sheddon, who died 1835 was buried in the Town Cemetery. His connection with William Chisholm is unknown.

SUMNER

William Johnson Sumner: proprietor of the Oakville House Hotel and an eminent resident of Oakville. He bought Park Lots on Dundas Street (Trafalgar Road) in the area of the street named after him.

THOMAS

Merrick Thomas: general manager of William Chisholm's shipyard and line of sailing ships. He was married in 1827 to Esther Silverthorn, sister of Mrs. William Chisholm. From 1833 he lived on his property at the southeast corner of Colborne and the street named after him (Lakeshore Road and Thomas Street).

WALKER

The Hon. William Walker: member of the legislative council of Lower Canada and head of the Quebec Branch of Forsyth, Richardson & Company.*

WILLIAM

Named for a member of the Chisholm family, probably for the founder himself.

WILSON

The brothers *Robert, William, and George Wilson*, all lake captains and friends of William Chisholm.

STREETS NAMED AT A LATER DATE — IN THE TOWNSHIP OF TRAFALGAR

CENTRE AVENUE (now Balsam Drive)

Named by William Wass, since it ran through the "centre" of his farm.

* See * p. 191.

MACDONALD ROAD

This area in the former Township of Trafalgar was the farm of the *MacDonald family*, whose house still stands at the northwest corner of this road and the Eighth Line (Chartwell Road).

MORRISON ROAD

Opened in 1912-13 through the former cattle farm of *William Morrison*.

RADIAL ROAD

The continuation of Rebecca Street from the town limits, running parallel with the *Radial Railway* to the Bronte Road. The name was retained after the tracks were removed, but in the 1950s "Radial Road" was renamed Rebecca Street.

STREETS NAMED IN THE FORMATION OF EACH NEW "SURVEY"

From 1900 to 1910 five areas were developed on the outskirts of the original town of Oakville. Streets and building-lots were drawn to plan by a professional surveyor in each case; hence the use of the word "Survey."

1850s - "ROMAIN" and "THOMPSON SMITH" SURVEYS

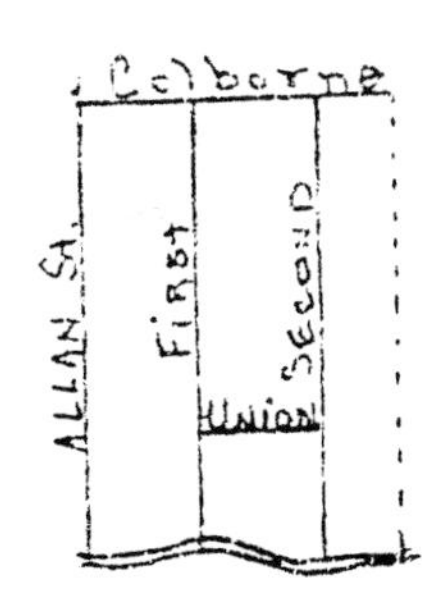

FIRST STREET
an access through the Romain Survey

SECOND STREET
an access through the Thompson Smith Survey

UNION STREET
connecting these two streets

1905-6 - "CARSON and BACON SURVEY"

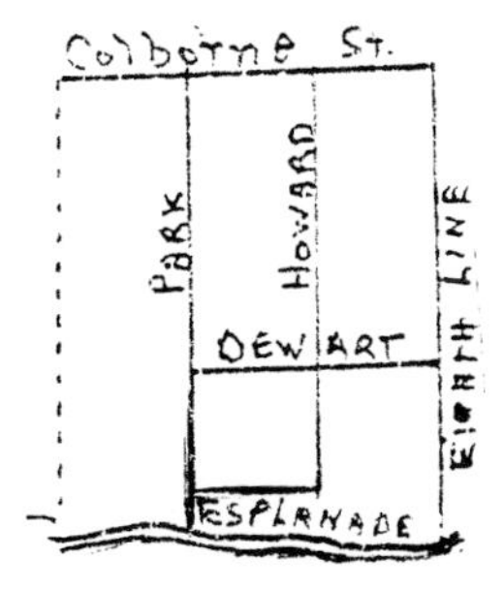

PARK AVENUE
ran as a lane, before this development, through a wooded area, Orchard Park, reaching the lake at Orchard Beach.

HOWARD AVENUE
DEWART STREET (now Carson Lane)
named for sons of Charles D. Carson

1907 - "BRANTWOOD SURVEY"

(a contraction of "Brant's Wood," named by C. W. Anderson because of his friendship with the descendants of Joseph Brant, chief of the Six Nations)

GLOUCESTER AVENUE
WATSON AVENUE
DOUGLAS AVENUE
GALT AVENUE
development of the former farm of C.W. Anderson by the Cumberland Land Company, Limited, and their agent W. S. Davis

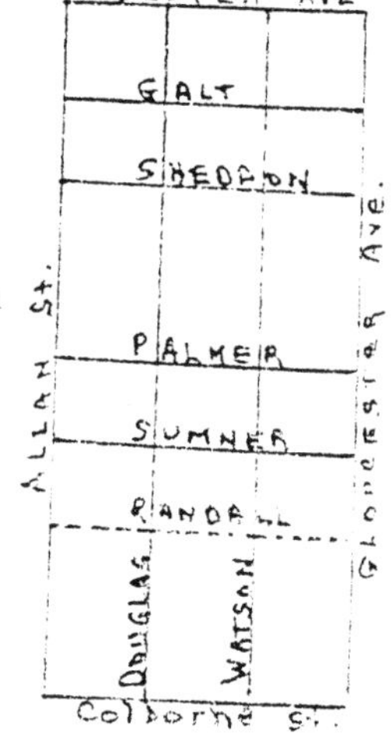

1909 - "INGLEHART SURVEY"

(developed by W.A. Inglehart from 37 acres of the former farm of John A. Chisholm Sr.)

INGLEHART AVENUE
opened in 1909 to provide building lots in W.A. Inglehart's new development

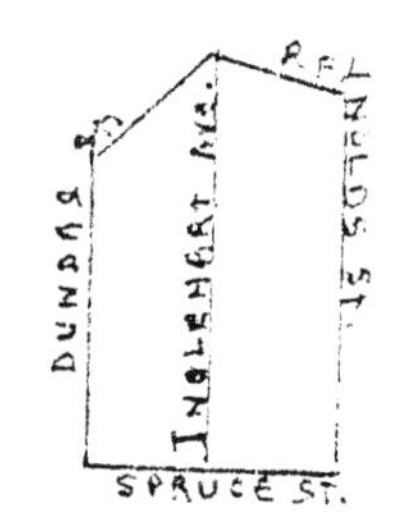

1910 - "TUXEDO PARK"

(developed on a part of the eastern section of the former Chisholm farm)

BELYEA AVENUE
SPRUCE STREET
MAPLE AVENUE
PINE AVENUE

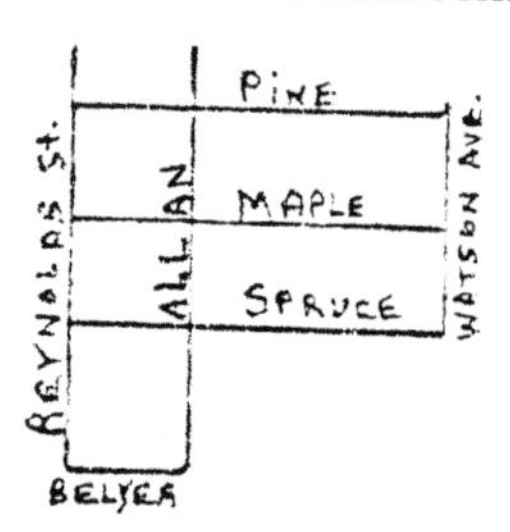

SCHOOLS

(See also chapter 6, "Educating the Young")

OAKVILLE "CENTRAL" SCHOOL

1828 - Oakville "Common" School
(Classes were held in a wooden meeting-hall at the west end of Church Street, which then ran through to the river bank.)

1850 - Oakville "Common" School
(brick building, west side of Navy, near Randall Street)

1871 - Oakville "Public" School (brick building, west side of Navy, near Randall Street)

1910 - Oakville "Central" School
(brick building west side of Navy, near Randall Street) renamed after removal of High School to Reynolds Street.

1950s New Central School (Balsam Drive, after demolition of Navy Street building.)

OAKVILLE HIGH SCHOOL

1853 - Oakville "Grammar" School
(with "Common" School, Navy Street)

1871 - Oakville "High" School
(with "Public" School, Navy Street)

1910 - Oakville "High" School
(new building, Reynolds Street)

1924 - Oakville "High" School
(A large addition to the school was completed in January of that year.)

1947 - Oakville-Trafalgar High School
(the high school district comprising the Town of Oakville was dissolved. The new district included the Town of Oakville and the Township of Trafalgar.)

ST. MARY'S SEPARATE SCHOOL

1860 - St. Mary's Separate School
(King Street at Allan)

1978 - École Ste. Marie
(total French immersion school)

MAPLE GROVE SCHOOL

1872 - Ninth Line School
(then Trafalgar School Section 12, on the present Maplegrove Drive.)

1930 - Maple Grove School
(renamed and enlarged on the same site)

PINE GROVE SCHOOL

1872 - Pine Grove School
(then Trafalgar School Section 18; now no.607 Stephens Crescent, east from the Fourth Line)

1956 - Pine Grove Public School
(new building, Fourth Line)

BRANTWOOD SCHOOL

1921 - Brantwood School
(named for the original "Brantwood Survey" on which it stands, on Allan Street)

WESTWOOD SCHOOL

1923 - Westwood School
(opened north side of Rebecca, between Wilson and Kerr streets)

1980 - Westwood School (closed)

LINBROOK SCHOOL

1933 - Linbrook School
(opened, north side of Linbrook Road)

PRIVATE SCHOOLS

1908 - Mrs. Sheldrake's School, southeast corner of King and Reynolds streets

1911 - Appleby School, two miles west of Oakville; renamed Appleby College March 5, 1941.

1912 - Miss Willis's School, Colborne Street, 2nd floor (approximate present location no.187 Lakeshore Road)

1914 - Miss Vera Crossley's School, Colborne Street, 2nd floor (same location)

1917 - Miss Creighton's School, Second Street (no.50)

1923 - Miss Lightbourn's School, Dunn Street (no.31)

1929 - Miss Lightbourn's School, Park Avenue (no.65)

1930 - Miss Lightborrn's School, Dundas Street (no.235 Trafalgar Road)

1937 - Miss Lightbourn's School, Reynolds Street (no.220)

1969 - Became St. Mildred's Lightbourn School, Linbrook Road (no.1080)

CHURCHES

1830s- 1869 - Methodist Episcopal, Wilson and John streets
1839 - 1841 - Wesleyan Methodist, Thomas and Colborne (Lakeshore Road)
1840 - St. Andrew's Roman Catholic, Reynolds and King Streets
1842 - 1884 - St. Jude's Church of England, Thomas and Colborne (Lakeshore Road)
1851 - 1878 - Wesleyan Methodist* southeast corner Dunn and Randall Streets
1850 - 1888 - Canada Presbyterian, William Street (nos.295-99)
1869 - 1878 - Methodist Episcopal* Navy and Randall Streets
1878 - St. John's Methodist, Dunn and Randall Streets
1884 - St. Jude's Church of England, Thomas and William Streets
1885 - Salvation army (meeting-halls)
1888 - Knox Presbyterian, Dunn and Colborne (Lakeshore Road)
1892 - African Methodist Episcopal, Colborne Street West (Lakeshore Road West)
1916 - Christian Science Congregation
1924 - St. John's Methodist became St. John's United after "Church Union" with a part of the Presbyterian congregation.

*In 1878 these two churches joined under the name of St. John's Methodist Church.

BANKS

1857 - 1860 - Bank of Toronto, Custom House building, Navy Street
1860 - 1871 - No bank in Oakville
1871 - 1884 - Private Bank of C. Tate Scott & Company
1881 - 1902 - Private Bank of Andrew & Haworth
1887 - 1902 - Private Bank of C.W. Anderson & Sons
1898 - Merchants Bank, northwest corner Thomas and Colborne (Lakeshore Road) (F.G. Oliver)

1902 - Bank of Toronto, Colborne Street (no.134 Lakeshore Road) (J.B.L. Grout)
1910 - Bank of Hamilton, Colborne Street (no.187 Lakeshore Road) (W.S. Davis)
1910 - Merchants Bank, new building on original site (F.G. Oliver; H.L. Read)
1922 - Bank of Montreal (amalgamated with Merchants Bank) (H.L. Read)
1922 - Bank of Toronto, new building, Thomas and Colborne Streets (J.B.L. Grout)
1922 - Royal Bank of Canada, corner Dundas street (Trafalgar Road) and Inglehart Avenue (I.N. Tompkins)
1923 - Canadian Bank of Commerce (amalgamated with Bank of Hamilton) (E.M. Paynter)

THE POST OFFICE

1835-1856 - *First Post Office*
west of Navy Street; now part of the Old Post Office Museum
1856-1889 - *Second Post Office*
north side of Lakeshore Road (approximate present location, no.185)
1889-1910 - *Third Post Office*
north side of Lakeshore Road in the Davis Building (no.187)
1910-1939 - *Fourth Post Office*
east half of the present no.221 Lakeshore Road
1939-1956 - *Fifth Post Office*
Stone building; present no.216 Lakeshore Road
1956-1958 - *(Temporary Quarters)*
Southwest corner of Dunn and Church Streets
1958 - *Sixth Post Office*
present Post Office Building, Church Street

THE LIBRARY

1839 - Establishment of a "Library for the Village of Oakville", one of the first libraries in Upper Canada.

1865 - Located on the second floor of the tower in the Common School (Central), Navy Street.

(1895) - (Became "Oakville Public Library," an "Association library.")

1903 - Located in two rooms over the old Bank of Toronto (no.134 Lakeshore Road).

1908 - Located in no.198 Lakeshore Road.

(1938) - (Became a "Free Public Library," supported by municipal and provincial grants.)

1956 - Located in the vacated stone Post Office Building (no.216 Lakeshore Road).

1967 - Located in the Centennial Library Building, Navy Street.

CUSTOMS COLLECTION

1834 - William Chisholm first established Oakville as a port of entry.

1854-1894 - R.K. Chisholm, first customs collector, built the Customs House, Navy Street.

1910 - New Customs Office established on the second floor of Louis Coté Building (no.221 Lakeshore Road).

1937 - Oakville closed as a port of entry.

Index